JOEL CONARROE

EIGHT AMERICAN POETS

The author of books and essays about American poetry and fiction and the editor of *Six American Poets*, Joel Conarroe is president of the John Simon Guggenheim Memorial Foundation, which awards fellowships to artists and scholars. He has previously served as chairman of the English department and dean of arts and sciences at the University of Pennsylvania and as executive director of the Modern Language Association. He has earned degrees from Davidson College, Cornell University, and New York University, and has been awarded honorary doctorates by several institutions.

ALSO BY JOEL CONARROE

John Berryman: An Introduction to the Poetry

William Carlos Williams' Paterson:
Language and Landscape

ANTHOLOGY

Six American Poets

EIGHT AMERICAN POETS

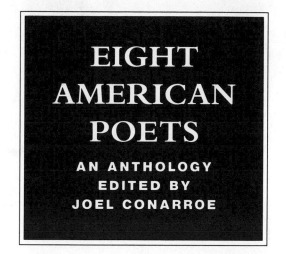

EIGHT AMERICAN POETS

**AN ANTHOLOGY
EDITED BY
JOEL CONARROE**

THEODORE ROETHKE

ELIZABETH BISHOP

ROBERT LOWELL

JOHN BERRYMAN

ANNE SEXTON

SYLVIA PLATH

ALLEN GINSBERG

JAMES MERRILL

VINTAGE BOOKS   A DIVISION OF RANDOM HOUSE, INC.   NEW YORK

3 1969 01234 1714

First Vintage Books Edition, March 1997

Copyright © 1994 by Joel Conarroe

All rights reserved under International and Pan-American Copyright
Conventions. Published in the United States by Vintage Books, a division of
Random House, Inc., New York, and simultaneously in Canada by Random
House of Canada Limited, Toronto. Originally published in hardcover by
Random House, Inc., New York, in 1994.

Owing to limitations of space, permission credits for previously published
material can be found on pages following Index of First Lines.

Photo credits:
Photo of Theodore Roethke is reproduced courtesy of Burt Glinn/Magnum
Photos. © Burt Glinn/Magnum Photos.
Photo of Elizabeth Bishop is reproduced courtesy of the photographer,
Rollie McKenna. © Rollie McKenna.
Photo of Robert Lowell is reproduced courtesy of Culver Pictures.
Photo of John Berryman is reproduced courtesy of the photographer, Tom
Berthiaume/Parallel Productions. © Tom Berthiaume/Parallel Productions.
Photo of Anne Sexton is reproduced courtesy of the photographer,
Rollie McKenna. © Rollie McKenna.
Photos of Sylvia Plath, Allen Ginsberg, and James Merrill are reproduced
courtesy of UPI/Bettmann.

The Library of Congress has cataloged the Random House edition as follows:

Eight American Poets: Theodore Roethke, Elizabeth Bishop, Robert Lowell,
John Berryman, Anne Sexton, Sylvia Plath, Allen Ginsberg, James Merrill :
an anthology / edited by Joel Conarroe.—1st ed.
p. cm.
Includes bibliographical references and index.
ISBN 0-679-42779-1
1. American poetry—20th century. I. Conarroe, Joel, 1934– .
PS613.E37 1994
811'.508—dc20   94-10186

Vintage ISBN: 0-679-77643-5

Random House Web address: http://www.randomhouse.com/

Printed in the United States of America
10 9 8 7

For
Robert Warner
and
Brigitte Weeks

ACKNOWLEDGMENTS

A number of friends and colleagues helped bring this anthology into being, some of them in ways they probably won't remember. I am especially grateful to Patricia O'Sullivan, Roslyn Schloss, William Pahlka, Jason Epstein, Jean-Isabel McNutt, Alice van Straalen, Benjamin Taylor, Fran and Howard Kiernan, Clare Maclean Scott and Frank Scott, Peter Kardon, Wendy Grace, Brad Leithauser, David Del Tredici, Neil Baldwin, Betty Comden, Claire Bloom, Joseph Roddy, Peter Conn, Cleo Tom, Joseph Brodsky, Andrew Carroll, John O'Conner, Louis and Anka Begley, Ophelia Davis, Chet Lenda, Jeffrey M. Perl, Ann Lucas, J. D. McClatchy, William Pritchard, Edward Hirsch, James and Janet and Matthew Sgritto, Juan Berrios, Matt Webb, Harry Brownlee, Eileen Darby, Fred Myers, Victor Tom, Dr. Nicholas Christy, the late Robert Savage, and the two irreplaceable individuals to whom the work is dedicated.

CONTENTS

INTRODUCTION

I had hoped to find a lyrical title for this anthology, one worthy of the eloquent work it contains, but none of the possibilities that came to mind quite fit the bill. I opted against "Wonder and Delight," for example, when a whimsical friend said the phrase conjured up a pair of trained circus dogs. That wouldn't do. I considered "Rough News," a term from the world of paper-making; it suggests the uncensored quality of much recent work and also plays on Ezra Pound's definition of poetry as "news that stays news." But that, too, ended on the discard pile—most of the poems I have selected are anything but rough, indeed are polished to a high gloss. "Songs of Myself" has a robust Whitmanian resonance that suits the book's confessional lyrics, but it's not sufficiently inclusive. "Kindred Spirits" seemed the answer to my quest until I discovered that the title is already in use—for a collection of gay science fiction. And while I like the mysterious sound of "Cages for Infinity," from a poem by Octavio Paz about Joseph Cornell, the phrase is a more imaginative description of Cornell's evocative assemblages than of this era's poems.

I finally settled on "Eight American Poets"—not exactly lyrical, to be sure, but certainly accurate. And perhaps this decidedly functional title was preordained, the book having been designed as a companion volume to *Six American Poets,* published in 1991. It was the heartening response to that collection of "classic" American poets—Whitman, Dickinson, Stevens, Williams, Frost, and Hughes—that encouraged those involved in its publication to think an anthology introducing this century's second brilliant generation might find a receptive audience as well. Thus, eight postmodern poets follow their six forebears—and the next volume will logically up the ante to ten.

"Heartening response," though, is not what typically greets collections of poetry, most of which prompt modest sales at best and then languish on the remainder shelf. A poet, Berryman complained, is someone who mounts a platform to give an address, "looks around, and finds the hall—empty." Or, as Don Marquis once observed, publishing a book of poetry in the United States is like dropping a rose petal into the Grand Canyon and waiting for an echo. *Six American Poets,* however, was twice blessed, first by being named a main selection of the Book-of-the-Month Club (the first collection of poetry so chosen in fifty-five years) and then by receiving the support of a Nobel laureate who has also been poet laureate of the United States. Joseph Brodsky, a political exile from his native Russia, believed passionately that American poetry is an undervalued treasure that ought to be found in hotel rooms, on airplanes, and anywhere else potential readers may happen to be. As a result of his vision and the efforts of his colleague Andrew Carroll, *Six American Poets* now awaits travelers in seemingly unlikely places across the country.

The present book's purpose is identical to that of the earlier collection: once again I introduce, through generous examples of their work, a limited number of important writers who do indeed bring news that stays news. My only source of frustration, as it was in the earlier book, which had no room for Marianne Moore, E. E. Cummings, and other worthy artists, has been the necessity to leave some exceptional singers out of the opera. Following the example of other anthologists, I could have included many more writers, but that would have meant a skimpier sampling, something at odds with my desire to provide the sort of substantial selection that will send a captivated audience in search of further reading. Any anthology is, of course, the product of its editor's taste, and I willingly take responsibility for all perceived sins of omission.

"A good poet," Randall Jarrell said, "is someone who manages, in a lifetime of standing out in thunderstorms, to be struck by lightning five or six times; a dozen or two dozen times and he is great." Needless to say, not every poet I have chosen, even though they have all been struck many times, is going to speed every reader to a bookstore or library. If, however, a few lifelong relationships are forged I will have accomplished my goal. All the same, I regret the exclusion of writers who have been among my boon companions over the years and who deserve an anthology all to themselves. Perhaps the future will indeed bring together ten American poets, followed eventually by an even dozen, collections that will include such admirable figures as Richard Wilbur, James Wright, Adrienne Rich, Philip Levine, John Ashbery, Mark Doty, Rita Dove, Edward Hirsch, and others equally deserving of a wide audience. In the meantime, I recommend *The Vintage Book of Contemporary Poetry,* edited by J. D. McClatchy, a poet who includes examples of work by no fewer than sixty-five writers.

The eight poets represented here, though they share certain traits and subjects, have voices that are distinctive. They all learned from others—in some cases from one another—but each one gradually transmuted those various sources into a unique style. Just as after hearing even a few bars of music one can identify the composer as, say, Aaron Copland or Leonard Bernstein, an attentive reader coming across lines by any of these poets would be able to say with some assurance, "That's Theodore Roethke," for example, or "That could only be Elizabeth Bishop." The clues lie not so much in subject matter as in rhythm, diction, syntax, and especially tone.

A poet (or a composer) is not, of course, born possessing an original style but typically goes through a period of apprenticeship, frequently echoing other voices. Anne Sexton and Sylvia Plath sat in on one of Robert Lowell's workshops, hence traces in their work of his unmistakable approach to language are not surprising. "He works with a cold chisel with no more mercy than a dentist," Sexton observed of Lowell. "But if he is never kind to the poem, he is kind to the poet." Sexton was also influenced by a host of other writers, including, importantly, W. D. Snodgrass; and Plath's work shows the imprint of Roethke in particular. Once they no longer deferred to their mentors, however, their use of language became strikingly original.

The web of literary and personal connections among these gifted men and women is well illustrated by the career of Lowell, not only as mentor to Plath and Sexton but in other ways as well. He was, for example, impressed by Elizabeth Bishop's "humorous commanding genius for picking up the unnoticed" and also attracted to the poet herself, about whom he had romantic illusions, even to the point of considering a marriage proposal. Bishop, for her part, though hostile to most self-revelation, admired her friend's personal narratives and sought to duplicate their expressiveness in her later style. She is the dedicatee of Lowell's most powerfully revealing poem, "Skunk Hour," written in response to "The Armadillo," which she had dedicated to him.

Lowell and John Berryman, "co-explorers," in A. Alvarez's words, "of risky psychological terrain," were also stimulated by each other's work, though the result was a fierce one-upmanship in which they vied to be the superior architect of long sequences; Berryman's 385 dream songs, for example, clearly influenced the 373 poems in Lowell's *Notebook*. Close friends, they were among each other's best readers—an essay called "Despondency and Madness" that Berryman wrote about "Skunk Hour" is dazzling, and Lowell's review of 77 *Dream Songs,* which he called "one of the glories of the age," is as perceptive a critique as Berryman received in his lifetime: "All is risk and variety here. This great Pierrot's universe is more tearful and funny than we can easily bear." Following Randall Jarrell's suicide, Lowell wrote Berryman: "This is really to say that I love you and wonder at you, and want you to take care. . . . If anything happened to you, I'd feel the heart of the scene had gone." The eulogy he later composed is moving: "Yet really we had the same life, / the generic one / our generation offered. . . . "

Lowell's letters reveal his belief that some sort of curse doomed his generation. "John B. in his mad way keeps talking about something evil stalking us poets," he wrote. "That's a bad way to talk, but there's truth to it." He discovered another kindred spirit in Roethke, not artistically—he found the work "a fairly small thing done, at best, with remarkable clarity and freshness"—but personally: both were afflicted with a manic-depressive condition that often resulted in hospitalization. (Elizabeth Hardwick called them "competitors in symptoms.") They got to know each other at Yaddo, an artists' colony, and later, despite feelings of rivalry, visited, read publicly together, and stayed in touch through the mail. Lowell's notes to Roethke (some addressed "Dear Bear"), like his messages to Berryman, are infused with an affectionate, almost fraternal concern.

As for Allen Ginsberg, in many ways an unlikely compatriot, it was precisely the differences that accounted for the connection. Lowell credits Ginsberg, among others, with the much-analyzed change in his style, a movement away from a kind of muscle-bound turgidity toward the clarity evident in the novel-istic confessions of *Life Studies,* which became the single most influential work of this half-century:

He was soon fired. Year after year,
he still hummed "Anchors Aweigh" in the tub—
whenever he left a job,
he bought a smarter car.
Father's last employer
was Scudder, Stevens and Clark, Investment Advisors,
himself his only client.
(from "Commander Lowell")

The heir of Blake, Whitman, and Williams, Ginsberg did not, for his part, fall under the spell of his brilliant contemporary—whom he called "America's leading poet"—even though they read together publicly and held similar views on a number of social issues. Born the same year as Ginsberg, James Merrill, too, though he shares with Lowell an obsession with history (and family history) and a deep knowledge of literature, was largely influenced by others, especially Auden, Stevens, and Bishop.

It has been shrewdly observed that poets are more likely to produce perfect poems than perfect lives. What alone constitutes life for a poet, according to T. S. Eliot, is the struggle "to transmute his personal and private agonies into something rich and strange, something universal and impersonal." The brief biographical introductions I provide for these eight artists reveal, with no attempt to soften the details, some decidedly grim patterns—mental breakdown, depression, institutionalization, alcoholism, and suicide. Other prominent figures of the period—notably Randall Jarrell, Delmore Schwartz, and Frank O'Hara—also lived close to the edge and died under troubling circumstances. And since he died on this side of the Atlantic, we could add to this terrible list the self-destructive Dylan Thomas. Berryman was outside the hospital room when Thomas died of an alcoholic "insult to the brain."

Even allowing for times when many conditions went undiagnosed, I find it hard to imagine a period of literary history in which so many major poets suffered such cataclysmic breakdowns. Schwartz, a close friend of Berryman and Lowell, stands as an extreme emblematic figure of the times. Blessed with extraordinary good looks and intellect, a brilliant talker and writer who won the coveted Bollingen Prize while he was still a young man, he died utterly alone in the seedy hotel off Times Square where he had spent his final months drinking and nursing paranoid obsessions. Fourteen of Berryman's dream songs stand as a grief-stricken eulogy to this tortured soulmate, and Lowell, too, mourned his "nobly mad" friend in anguished verse.

We are bound to wonder what it was about this generation of gifted creators that rendered them so vulnerable. To be sure, art usually exists at several removes from its creator, and even a disciplined imaginative writer is also, in Yeats's words, "a bundle contemporary examples seem. Plato believed a poet is incapable of composing "until he becomes inspired, and, as it were, mad, or whilst any reason remains in him," and Aristotle wondered why "all men who are outstanding in philosophy, poetry, or the arts are melancholic." In the seventeenth century, John Dryden penned an often-quoted couplet: "Great wits are sure to madness near allied, / And thin partitions do their bounds divide." In the last century Nietzsche declared that "one must still have chaos in oneself to be able to give birth to a dancing star," and the sculptor Augustus Saint-Gaudens observed that "what garlic is to salad, insanity is to art." "In relation to Gauguin, Van Gogh and Rimbaud," Jean-Paul Sartre wrote in our own time, "I have a distinct inferiority complex because they managed to destroy themselves. . . . I am more and more convinced that, in order to achieve authenticity, something has to snap."

It has recently been suggested, by reputable researchers, that there may well be a link between certain disturbances and creative achievement and that artists are unusually susceptible to major depressions. It is startling to note that the list of major writers who suffered from manic-depressive conditions includes—in addition to Lowell and Roethke—Byron, Shelley, Coleridge, Melville, and Woolf. "There is something I am convinced in the poetical temperament," Byron wrote, "that precludes happiness, not only to the person who has it, but to those connected with him." Psychiatrists have compiled persuasive evidence that, among especially gifted individuals, both manic-depressive illness and major depression are ten to thirty times as prevalent as in the general population. All the same, the incidence of depression among the leading poets of this half-century, nothing short of a plague, is extraordinary.

Whatever the causes, the tragic implications for what is sometimes called the middle generation were not lost on its poets themselves, who, as they saw one after another of their number suffer the debilitating effects of mental distress, clearly did not hold cheap the "cliffs of fall." Lowell speculated on the disturbing pattern in a letter to Roethke: "There's a strange fact about the poets of roughly our age," he wrote, "and one that doesn't exactly seem to have been always true. It's this, that to write we seem to have to go at it with such single-minded intensity that we are always on the point of drowning. . . . I feel it's something almost unavoidable, some flaw in the motor. . . . I can see us all being written up in some huge book of the age. But under what title?"

Just before she died, Elizabeth Bishop drafted a snappish letter to John Frederick Nims, who was preparing an anthology for college use that featured interpretive footnotes. "I think anyone who gets as far as college should be able to use a dictionary," she said. "If a poem catches a student's interest at all, he or she should damned well be able to look up an unfamiliar word in the dictionary." She is right, of course: a dictionary, like an encyclopedia, is an indispensable companion for any reader, whether of poetry or of prose. Obstacles other than unfamiliar words may still stand between a reader and a poem, but a dictionary can at least clarify individual passages and thus help release a work's overall melody.

Following my practice in *Six American Poets,* I once again let the poets speak for themselves, including only such notes as they themselves provide. Much of the literature written during this half-century is not immediately accessible, but as Helen Vendler has observed, writing that is both genuine and genuinely talented will eventually be understood. My own experience has persuaded me that an especially effective way to get a firm grip on lines of poetry, be they obscure or lucid, is to read them over and over, preferably aloud, until they lodge firmly in the mind, like those song lyrics we hear repeatedly during adolescence and remember all our lives.

While some poets reveal their secrets slowly, others will retain a degree of mystery, frustrating even the most conscientious efforts at interpretation, especially if one is intent on discovering literal meanings or paraphrasable content. "If the meaning of a poem is its essential characteristic," Wallace Stevens wrote a reader seeking the "solution" to an ambiguous lyric, "people would be putting themselves to a lot of trouble about nothing to set the meaning in a poetic form." Unfortunately, as that incisive gadfly Randall Jarrell pointedly observed, poets live in a world "where newspapers and magazines and books and motion pictures and radio stations and television stations have destroyed, in a great many people, even the capacity for understanding real poetry." The work in this volume is undeniably more challenging than magazines or television programs; many of these poems call not only for patience but also for imaginative collaboration, a strong and agile engagement with the words that will lift them off the inert page and give them life.

At its most effective, John Keats shrewdly observed, poetry will strike a reader "as a wording of his own highest thoughts, and appear almost a remembrance." One should not feel discouraged if a work, far from seeming a remembrance, remains, even after repeated readings, a haunting riddle. Experienced readers often find themselves puzzled by a phrase, a line, indeed an entire lyric. But perseverance will invariably bring a flash of insight and, with it, the nameless pleasure of possessing, of calling one's own, a complex work of art. In a sequence called "January Morning," William Carlos Williams, addressing his mother, describes this challenge:

> All this—
>   was for you, old woman.
> I wanted to write a poem
> That you would understand.
> For what good is it to me
> If you can't understand it?
>   But you got to try hard—

The following general works offer especially valuable insights into the poetry of this half-century: Bruce Bawer, *The Middle Generation: The Lives and Poetry of Delmore Schwartz, Randall Jarrell, John Berryman, and Robert Lowell* (Archon Books, 1986); Richard Howard, *Alone with America: Essays on the Art of Poetry* in *America since 1950* (Atheneum, 1969); Karl Malkoff, *Crowell's Handbook of Contemporary American Poetry* (Thomas Y. Crowell Co., 1973); Jeffrey Meyers, *Manic Power: Robert Lowell and His Circle* (Arbor House, 1987); Anne Middleton, "What Was Confessional Poetry?" in *The Columbia History of American Poetry* (Columbia University Press, 1993); David Perkins, *A History of Modern Poetry* (Harvard University Press, 1987); Robert Phillips, *The Confessional Poets* (Southern Illinois University Press, 1973); M. L. Rosenthal, *Our Life in Poetry: Selected Essays and Reviews* (Persea Books, 1991); Eileen Simpson, *Poets in Their Youth* (Random House, 1982); Helen Vendler, *The Music of What Happens: Poems, Poets, Critics* (Harvard University Press, 1988).

THEODORE ROETHKE

His friends liked to refer to him as the dancing bear. A man of enormous appetites as well as enormous gifts, Theodore Roethke was physically imposing, standing over six foot three and weighing in at more than 200 pounds. He had a lumbering gait and, like Walt Whitman, thought of himself as "one of the roughs," a man as much at home with laborers as with intellectuals. What our country needs, he said, is more barnyard poets—there isn't time for good taste, and besides, poetry requires a certain vulgarity, even brutality, to communicate the "aliveness of life." He had little patience for the "hyenas of sensibility, anglo-saxon apostles of refinement" who would turn the house of poetry into a museum. At one point he penned the following to "Pipling," a critic:

> He heaps few honors on a living head;
> He loves himself, and the illustrious dead;
> He pipes, he squeaks, he quivers through his nose,—
> Some cannot praise him: *I* am one of those.

Seeing himself as an undereducated bull in the china shop of academic literature, Roethke balked at being appropriated by the cultural establishment, the "tweed-coated cliché-masters." In London, riding with his wife in a Rolls-Royce, he leaned over and passed her a note: "Don't act impressed." With his Charles Laughton looks, his devotion to strong drink, and his unabashed sensuality, he has been variously described as Minnesota Fats with an Underwood and as a chalk-in-hand sot, drawing faces on the barroom floor.

The advocate of blunt honesty who railed against overrefined taste was, in fact, the gentlest of giants, whose lyrics reveal a delicacy of spirit utterly at odds with his sometimes gross public persona. Engaged in a lifetime love affair with the tiniest, most fragile inhabitants of the natural world ("I could say hello to things," he declared), this robust man who counted himself "among the happy poets" would fall on his knees and weep when he had brought forth a poem that he knew was good. In the words of critic Herbert Leibowitz, "He was uncannily alive to, and attracted by, a dark kingdom of slugs, molds, worms and stones where the will was nearly extinguished. Yet he was as attentive as Thoreau at Walden Pond to the swelling bud." Like two of his father figures, Walt Whitman and Wallace Stevens, he had the rare ability to make his readers experience the joy of simply being alive.

Roethke's biography, however, is hardly a history of unalloyed joy. In addition to alcoholism, with its periodic debilitating binges, he suffered from a manic condition that led to awful episodes (he was once removed from his classroom in handcuffs) and periods in institutions. "What's madness," he wrote, "but nobility of soul / at odds with circumstance?" His manic highs and bouts of schizophrenia became increasingly severe as he got older, but thanks to the esteem in which he was held at the University of Washington, where he taught for the last fifteen years of his life, arrangements were made for discreet leaves of absence. He wrote constantly, usually in a state of great excitement, but his superhuman energy was clearly a mixed blessing, deriving, at least in part, from his incurable condition.

The senior member of this anthology, Roethke was born in Saginaw, Michigan, on May 25, 1908. His informal education, invaluable to a writer so much in tune with the rhythms of the natural world, took place before he left home for college. His father and uncle owned a twenty-five-acre complex of greenhouses, and it was here that he experienced the formative emotional connection that was later transmuted into sensuous, ecstatic, and intensely interior poems. "When I wanted a job," he said, "they'd always give me good dirty work to do."

And I think of roses, roses,
White and red, in the wide six-hundred-foot greenhouses,
And my father standing astride the cement benches,
Lifting me high over the four-foot stems, the Mrs. Russells,
    and his own elaborate hybrids,
And how those flowerheads seemed to flow toward me, to
    beckon me, only a child, out of myself.

During the boy's fourteenth year his authoritarian father, Otto, died of cancer, and this loss, coupled with the earlier suicide of his uncle (recently estranged from Otto), left him with feelings of guilt and abandonment that were to haunt him throughout his life.

After earning a bachelor's degree at the University of Michigan, he entered the university's law school, but soon transferred to Harvard for graduate work. ("I came complete with fur coat and fancy suit. Those Harvards weren't going to have it over me.") It was during this period, at age twenty-one, that he began to write, encouraged by the poet Robert Hillyer. He completed a master's degree and took a position at Lafayette College, teaching English and coaching the tennis team.

He went on to teach at Penn State, Bennington College, and finally the University of Washington, where he was named a full professor in 1948 and later poet in residence. In 1953 he married a former student, Beatrice Heath O'Connell. By all accounts an inspiring classroom presence, Roethke made poetry live and breathe for the young men and women under his tutelage. "Those students get the highest grades," he wrote, "who take their responsibilities of educating me most seriously."

His first book, *Open House,* appeared in 1941, in his thirty-third year, and though echoing Auden, Frost, and other models, it introduced the rich music, fine, bitter wit, and dramatic themes— Rabelaisian sensuality, terror and delight, cruelty and tenderness—that would characterize his work for the next twenty years.

In reviewing the book, Auden wrote that "many people have the experience of feeling physically soiled and humiliated by life. . . . Both to remember and to transform the humiliation into something beautiful, as Mr. Roethke does, is rare." *The Lost Son and Other Poems,* seven years later, attracted even more critical praise, largely because of an irresistible sequence of thirteen "greenhouse" lyrics that dramatize the poet's empathy (and quest for oneness) with all animate life: "I can hear, underground, that sucking and sobbing, / In my veins, in my bones I feel it."

Other intense and moving books, all with evocative titles, appeared regularly—*Praise to the End,* a sequence of dramatic pieces, in 1951; *The Waking* in 1953; and *Words for the Wind: The Collected Verse* in 1958. A posthumous collection, though uneven in quality, contains a memorable "North American Sequence," philosophic lyrics that seem to foreshadow the poet's impending death as he approaches "this last place of light."

Roethke also published a collection of charming nonsense verse (and some not so nonsensical), *I Am! Says the Lamb,* suggestive of both A. A. Milne and Lewis Carroll. At his death he left 277 notebooks, the jottings and rough drafts of a twenty-year obsession with images and sounds. Selected and arranged by David Wagoner, these observations and notes, published under the title *Straw for the Fire,* reveal the distance between raw material (a poet's compost heap) and finished verse. This intuitive man who could sing like an angel ("I knew a woman, lovely in her bones") was also capable of such howlers as "In the ponds of her being I was the happiest fish," and "I'm surrounded by the lint from an enormous navel," insights, fortunately, that did not find their way into the poetry.

At the time of his death, the poet had gained celebrity for his legendary public readings and had also won a Pulit--- ..ze, two National Book Awards, the Bollinge- * ..u, a Guggenheim Fellowship, and a Fulbright lecturesnip (taken in Italy). In 1959, moreover, along with Saul Bellow, E. E. Cummings, and Flannery O'Connor, he received one of the first Ford Foundation grants to creative artists. No amount of public approbation, however, could retard his private dissolution, both spiritual and physical. In 1963, while visiting a friend on Puget Sound, he waded into a swimming pool where he was later found face-down in the water, dead of a heart attack. He was only fifty-five.

The Collected Poems of Theodore Roethke (Anchor Doubleday, 1975). Allan Seager, *The Glass House: The Life of Theodore Roethke* (McGraw-Hill, 1968). For criticism, see Karl Malkoff, *Theodore Roethke: An Introduction to the Poetry* (Columbia University Press, 1966), and Jenijoy LaBelle, *The Echoing Wood of Theodore Roethke* (Princeton University Press, 1976).

PRAYER

If I must of my Senses lose,
I pray Thee, Lord, that I may choose
Which of the Five I shall retain
Before oblivion clouds the brain.
My Tongue is generations dead,
My Nose defiles a comely head;
For hearkening to carnal evils
My Ears have been the very devil's.
And some have held the Eye to be
The instrument of lechery,
More furtive than the Hand in low
And vicious venery—Not so!
Its rape is gentle, never more
Violent than a metaphor.
In truth, the Eye's the abettor of
The holiest platonic love:
Lip, Breast and Thigh cannot possess
So singular a blessedness.
Therefore, O Lord, let me preserve
The Sense that does so fitly serve,
Take Tongue and Ear—all else I have—
Let Light attend me to the grave!

THE BAT

By day the bat is cousin to the mouse.
He likes the attic of an aging house.

His fingers make a hat about his head.
His pulse beat is so slow we think him dead.

He loops in crazy figures half the night
Among the trees that face the corner light.

But when he brushes up against a screen,
We are afraid of what our eyes have seen:

For something is amiss or out of place
When mice with wings can wear a human face.

CUTTINGS

Sticks-in-a-drowse droop over sugary loam,
Their intricate stem-fur dries;
But still the delicate slips keep coaxing up water;
The small cells bulge;

One nub of growth
Nudges a sand-crumb loose,
Pokes through a musty sheath
Its pale tendrilous horn.

CUTTINGS

(later)

This urge, wrestle, resurrection of dry sticks,
Cut stems struggling to put down feet,

What saint strained so much,
Rose on such lopped limbs to a new life?

I can hear, underground, that sucking and sobbing,
In my veins, in my bones I feel it,—
The small waters seeping upward,
The tight grains parting at last.
When sprouts break out,
Slippery as fish,
I quail, lean to beginnings, sheath-wet.

WEED PULLER

Under the concrete benches,
Hacking at black hairy roots,—
Those lewd monkey-tails hanging from drainholes,—
Digging into the soft rubble underneath,
Webs and weeds,
Grubs and snails and sharp sticks,
Or yanking tough fern-shapes,
Coiled green and thick, like dripping smilax,
Tugging all day at perverse life:
The indignity of it!—
With everything blooming above me,
Lilies, pale-pink cyclamen, roses,
Whole fields lovely and inviolate,—
Me down in that fetor of weeds,
Crawling on all fours,
Alive, in a slippery grave.

ORCHIDS

They lean over the path,
Adder-mouthed,
Swaying close to the face,

Coming out, soft and deceptive,
Limp and damp, delicate as a young bird's tongue;
Their fluttery fledgling lips
Move slowly,
Drawing in the warm air.

And at night,
The faint moon falling through whitewashed glass,
The heat going down
So their musky smell comes even stronger,
Drifting down from their mossy cradles:
So many devouring infants!
Soft luminescent fingers,
Lips neither dead nor alive,
Loose ghostly mouths
Breathing.

BIG WIND

Where were the greenhouses going,
Lunging into the lashing
Wind driving water
So far down the river
All the faucets stopped?—
So we drained the manure-machine
For the steam plant,
Pumping the stale mixture
Into the rusty boilers,
Watching the pressure gauge
Waver over to red,
As the seams hissed
And the live steam
Drove to the far
End of the rose-house,
Where the worst wind was,
Creaking the cypress window-frames,

Cracking so much thin glass
We stayed all night,
Stuffing the holes with burlap;
But she rode it out,
That old rose-house,
She hove into the teeth of it,
The core and pith of that ugly storm,
Ploughing with her stiff prow,
Bucking into the wind-waves
That broke over the whole of her,
Flailing her sides with spray,
Flinging long strings of wet across the roof-top,
Finally veering, wearing themselves out, merely
Whistling thinly under the wind-vents;
She sailed until the calm morning,
Carrying her full cargo of roses.

CHILD ON TOP OF A GREENHOUSE

The wind billowing out the seat of my britches,
My feet crackling splinters of glass and dried putty,
The half-grown chrysanthemums staring up like accusers,
Up through the streaked glass, flashing with sunlight,
A few white clouds all rushing eastward,
A line of elms plunging and tossing like horses,
And everyone, everyone pointing up and shouting!

FRAU BAUMAN, FRAU SCHMIDT, AND FRAU SCHWARTZE

Gone the three ancient ladies
Who creaked on the greenhouse ladders,
Reaching up white strings
To wind, to wind

The sweet-pea tendrils, the smilax,
Nasturtiums, the climbing
Roses, to straighten
Carnations, red
Chrysanthemums; the stiff
Stems, jointed like corn,
They tied and tucked,—
These nurses of nobody else.
Quicker than birds, they dipped
Up and sifted the dirt;
They sprinkled and shook;
They stood astride pipes,
Their skirts billowing out wide into tents,
Their hands twinkling with wet;
Like witches they flew along rows
Keeping creation at ease;
With a tendril for needle
They sewed up the air with a stem;
They teased out the seed that the cold kept asleep,—
All the coils, loops, and whorls.
They trellised the sun; they plotted for more than themselves.

I remember how they picked me up, a spindly kid,
Pinching and poking my thin ribs
Till I lay in their laps, laughing,
Weak as a whiffet;
Now, when I'm alone and cold in my bed,
They still hover over me,
These ancient leathery crones,
With their bandannas stiffened with sweat,
And their thorn-bitten wrists,
And their snuff-laden breath blowing lightly over me in my
    first sleep.

My Papa's Waltz

The whiskey on your breath
Could make a small boy dizzy;
But I hung on like death:
Such waltzing was not easy.

We romped until the pans
Slid from the kitchen shelf;
My mother's countenance
Could not unfrown itself.

The hand that held my wrist
Was battered on one knuckle;
At every step you missed
My right ear scraped a buckle.

You beat time on my head
With a palm caked hard by dirt,
Then waltzed me off to bed
Still clinging to your shirt.

Pickle Belt

The fruit rolled by all day.
They prayed the cogs would creep;
They thought about Saturday pay,
And Sunday sleep.

Whatever he smelled was good:
The fruit and flesh smells mixed.
There beside him she stood,—
And he, perplexed;

He, in his shrunken britches,
Eyes rimmed with pickle dust,

Prickling with all the itches
Of sixteen-year-old lust.

THE MINIMAL

I study the lives on a leaf: the little
Sleepers, numb nudgers in cold dimensions,
Beetles in caves, newts, stone-deaf fishes,
Lice tethered to long limp subterranean weeds,
Squirmers in bogs,
And bacterial creepers
Wriggling through wounds
Like elvers in ponds,
Their wan mouths kissing the warm sutures,
Cleaning and caressing,
Creeping and healing.

THE WAKING

I strolled across
An open field;
The sun was out;
Heat was happy.

This way! This way!
The wren's throat shimmered,
Either to other,
The blossoms sang.

The stones sang,
The little ones did,
And flowers jumped
Like small goats.

A ragged fringe
Of daisies waved;

I wasn't alone
In a grove of apples.

Far in the wood
A nestling sighed;
The dew loosened
Its morning smells.

I came where the river
Ran over stones:
My ears knew
An early joy.

And all the waters
Of all the streams
Sang in my veins
That summer day.

THE VISITANT

1

A cloud moved close. The bulk of the wind shifted.
A tree swayed over water.
A voice said:
Stay. Stay by the slip-ooze. Stay.

Dearest tree, I said, may I rest here?
A ripple made a soft reply.
I waited, alert as a dog.
The leech clinging to a stone waited;
And the crab, the quiet breather.

2

Slow, slow as a fish she came,
Slow as a fish coming forward,
Swaying in a long wave;

Her skirts not touching a leaf,
Her white arms reaching towards me.

She came without sound,
Without brushing the wet stones,
In the soft dark of early evening,
She came,
The wind in her hair,
The moon beginning.

3

I woke in the first of morning.
Staring at a tree, I felt the pulse of a stone.

Where's she now, I kept saying.
Where's she now, the mountain's downy girl?

But the bright day had no answer.
A wind stirred in a web of appleworms;
The tree, the close willow, swayed.

ELEGY FOR JANE

MY STUDENT, THROWN BY A HORSE

I remember the neckcurls, limp and damp as tendrils;
And her quick look, a sidelong pickerel smile;
And how, once startled into talk, the light syllables leaped for
    her,
And she balanced in the delight of her thought,
A wren, happy, tail into the wind,
Her song trembling the twigs and small branches.
The shade sang with her;
The leaves, their whispers turned to kissing;
And the mold sang in the bleached valleys under the rose.

Oh, when she was sad, she cast herself down into such a pure
    depth,

Even a father could not find her:
Scraping her cheek against straw;
Stirring the clearest water.

My sparrow, you are not here,
Waiting like a fern, making a spiny shadow.
The sides of wet stones cannot console me,
Nor the moss, wound with the last light.

If only I could nudge you from this sleep,
My maimed darling, my skittery pigeon.
Over this damp grave I speak the words of my love:
I, with no rights in this matter,
Neither father nor lover.

ALL THE EARTH, ALL THE AIR

1

I stand with standing stones.
The stones stay where they are.
The twiny winders wind;
The little fishes move.
A ripple wakes the pond.

2

This joy's my fall. I am!—
A man rich as a cat,
A cat in the fork of a tree,
When she shakes out her hair.
I think of that, and laugh.

3

All innocence and wit,
She keeps my wishes warm;
When, easy as a beast,
She steps along the street,
I start to leave myself.

4

The truly beautiful,
Their bodies cannot lie:
The blossom stings the bee.
The ground needs the abyss,
Say the stones, say the fish.

5

A field recedes in sleep.
Where are the dead? Before me
Floats a single star.
A tree glides with the moon.
The field is mine! Is mine!

6

In a lurking-place I lurk,
One with the sullen dark.
What's hell but a cold heart?
But who, faced with her face,
Would not rejoice?

I KNEW A WOMAN

I knew a woman, lovely in her bones,
When small birds sighed, she would sigh back at them;
Ah, when she moved, she moved more ways than one:
The shapes a bright container can contain!
Of her choice virtues only gods should speak,
Or English poets who grew up on Greek
(I'd have them sing in chorus, cheek to cheek).

How well her wishes went! She stroked my chin,
She taught me Turn, and Counter-turn, and Stand;
She taught me Touch, that undulant white skin;
I nibbled meekly from her proffered hand;
She was the sickle; I, poor I, the rake,

Coming behind her for her pretty sake
(But what prodigious mowing we did make).

Love likes a gander, and adores a goose:
Her full lips pursed, the errant note to seize;
She played it quick, she played it light and loose;
My eyes, they dazzled at her flowing knees;
Her several parts could keep a pure repose,
Or one hip quiver with a mobile nose
(She moved in circles, and those circles moved).

Let seed be grass, and grass turn into hay:
I'm martyr to a motion not my own;
What's freedom for? To know eternity.
I swear she cast a shadow white as stone.
But who would count eternity in days?
These old bones live to learn her wanton ways:
(I measure time by how a body sways).

THE SURLY ONE

1

When true love broke my heart in half,
I took the whiskey from the shelf,
And told my neighbors when to laugh.
I keep a dog, and bark myself.

2

Ghost cries out to ghost—
But who's afraid of that?
I fear those shadows most
That start from my own feet.

THE WHALE

There was a most Monstrous Whale:
He had no Skin, he had no Tail.
When he tried to Spout, that Great Big Lubber,
The best he could do was Jiggle his Blubber.

THE DONKEY

I had a Donkey, that was all right,
But he always wanted to fly my Kite;
Every time I let him, the String would bust.
Your Donkey is better behaved, I trust.

THE HIPPO

A Head or Tail—which does he lack?
I think his Forward's coming back!
He lives on Carrots, Leeks and Hay;
He starts to yawn—it takes All Day—

Some time I think I'll live that way.

THE LONGING

1

On things asleep, no balm:
A kingdom of stinks and sighs,
Fetor of cockroaches, dead fish, petroleum,
Worse than castoreum of mink or weasels,
Saliva dripping from warm microphones,
Agony of crucifixion on barstools.

Less and less the illuminated lips,
Hands active, eyes cherished;
Happiness left to dogs and children—
(Matters only a saint mentions!)
Lust fatigues the soul.
How to transcend this sensual emptiness?
(Dreams drain the spirit if we dream too long.)
In a bleak time, when a week of rain is a year,
The slag-heaps fume at the edge of the raw cities:
The gulls wheel over their singular garbage;
The great trees no longer shimmer;
Not even the soot dances.

And the spirit fails to move forward,
But shrinks into a half-life, less than itself,
Falls back, a slug, a loose worm
Ready for any crevice,
An eyeless starer.

2

A wretch needs his wretchedness. Yes.
O pride, thou art a plume upon whose head?

How comprehensive that felicity! . . .
A body with the motion of a soul.
What dream's enough to breathe in? A dark dream.
The rose exceeds, the rose exceeds us all.
Who'd think the moon could pare itself so thin?
A great flame rises from the sunless sea;
The light cries out, and I am there to hear—
I'd be beyond; I'd be beyond the moon,
Bare as a bud, and naked as a worm.

To this extent I'm a stalk.
    —How free; how all alone.
Out of these nothings
    —All beginnings come.

3

I would with the fish, the blackening salmon, and the mad
    lemmings,
The children dancing, the flowers widening.
Who sighs from far away?
I would unlearn the lingo of exasperation, all the distortions
    of malice and hatred;
I would believe my pain: and the eye quiet on the growing
    rose;
I would delight in my hands, the branch singing, altering the
    excessive bird;
I long for the imperishable quiet at the heart of form;
I would be a stream, winding between great striated rocks in
    late summer;
A leaf, I would love the leaves, delighting in the redolent
    disorder of this mortal life,
This ambush, this silence,
Where shadow can change into flame,
And the dark be forgotten.
I have left the body of the whale, but the mouth of the night
    is still wide;
On the Bullhead, in the Dakotas, where the eagles eat well,
In the country of few lakes, in the tall buffalo grass at the
    base of the clay buttes,
In the summer heat, I can smell the dead buffalo,
The stench of their damp fur drying in the sun,
The buffalo chips drying.

Old men should be explorers?
I'll be an Indian.
Ogalala?
Iroquois.

HER LONGING

Before this longing,
I lived serene as a fish,
At one with the plants in the pond,
The mare's tail, the floating frogbit,
Among my eight-legged friends,
Open like a pool, a lesser parsnip,
Like a leech, looping myself along,
A bug-eyed edible one,
A mouth like a stickleback,—
A thing quiescent!

But now—
The wild stream, the sea itself cannot contain me:
I dive with the black hag, the cormorant,
Or walk the pebbly shore with the humpbacked heron,
Shaking out my catch in the morning sunlight,
Or rise with the gar-eagle, the great-winged condor.
Floating over the mountains,
Pitting my breast against the rushing air,
A phoenix, sure of my body,
Perpetually rising out of myself,
My wings hovering over the shorebirds,
Or beating against the black clouds of the storm,
Protecting the sea-cliffs.

ELEGY

Her face like a rain-beaten stone on the day she rolled off
With the dark hearse, and enough flowers for an alderman,—
And so she was, in her way, Aunt Tilly.

Sighs, sighs, who says they have sequence?
Between the spirit and the flesh,—what war?

She never knew;
For she asked no quarter and gave none,
Who sat with the dead when the relatives left,
Who fed and tended the infirm, the mad, the epileptic,
And, with a harsh rasp of a laugh at herself,
Faced up to the worst.

I recall how she harried the children away all the late summer
From the one beautiful thing in her yard, the peachtree;
How she kept the wizened, the fallen, the misshapen for
    herself,
And picked and pickled the best, to be left on rickety
    doorsteps.

And yet she died in agony,
Her tongue, at the last, thick, black as an ox's.

Terror of cops, bill collectors, betrayers of the poor,—
I see you in some celestial supermarket,
Moving serenely among the leeks and cabbages,
Probing the squash,
Bearing down, with two steady eyes,
On the quaking butcher.

THE MEADOW MOUSE

1

In a shoe box stuffed in an old nylon stocking
Sleeps the baby mouse I found in the meadow,
Where he trembled and shook beneath a stick
Till I caught him up by the tail and brought him in,
Cradled in my hand,
A little quaker, the whole body of him trembling,
His absurd whiskers sticking out like a cartoon-mouse,
His feet like small leaves,
Little lizard-feet,

Whitish and spread wide when he tried to struggle away,
Wriggling like a minuscule puppy.

Now he's eaten his three kinds of cheese and drunk from his
   bottle-cap watering-trough—
So much he just lies in one corner,
His tail curled under him, his belly big
As his head; his bat-like ears
Twitching, tilting toward the least sound.

Do I imagine he no longer trembles
When I come close to him?
He seems no longer to tremble.

2

But this morning the shoe-box house on the back porch is
   empty.
Where has he gone, my meadow mouse,
My thumb of a child that nuzzled in my palm?—
To run under the hawk's wing,
Under the eye of the great owl watching from the elm-tree,
To live by courtesy of the shrike, the snake, the tom-cat.

I think of the nestling fallen into the deep grass,
The turtle gasping in the dusty rubble of the highway,
The paralytic stunned in the tub, and the water rising,—
All things innocent, hapless, forsaken.

WISH FOR A YOUNG WIFE

My lizard, my lively writher,
May your limbs never wither,
May the eyes in your face
Survive the green ice
Of envy's mean gaze;

May you live out your life
Without hate, without grief,
And your hair ever blaze,
In the sun, in the sun,
When I am undone,
When I am no one.

Heard in a Violent Ward

In heaven, too,
You'd be institutionalized.
But that's all right,—
If they let you eat and swear
With the likes of Blake,
And Christopher Smart,
And that sweet man, John Clare.

ELIZABETH BISHOP

James Merrill once began a reading by dedicating a poem "to Elizabeth Bishop, our principal national treasure." This affectionate homage reflects an opinion shared by other poets about a painstaking perfectionist described by John Ashbery as a writer's writer's writer. The roster of Elizabeth Bishop's admirers includes Robert Lowell, Marianne Moore, Octavio Paz, Pablo Neruda, and scores of writers (and writer's writers) who compose under the spell of her clear-seeing, unpretentious art. Although showered with honors during her lifetime, this unassuming woman has only in the last decade or so come to be regarded as perhaps the most significant and enduring poet of her generation.

A private individual who made no headlines, published relatively little, avoided literary circles, and created work that is spectacular largely by virtue of being so unspectacular, Elizabeth Bishop seems an unlikely candidate for such canonization. The words that come to mind about her art hardly suggest literary dominance: dispassionate, selective, meticulous, reticent, disciplined, self-possessed, deliberate, whimsical, understated, accurate, fastidious, controlled, painterly. It is precisely, however, the seemingly artless naturalness and honesty of her plainspoken work—work that reveals both the "prose virtues" and what Marianne Moore called an unmannered originality of simplicity—that account for her high standing not only with other artists but with general readers as well.

Unwilling to publish so much as a phrase that did not meet

her exacting standards, she gradually created, in Richard Eberhart's words, "a rich world of slow, curious, strong discoveries, uniquely seen and set." Unlike her friend Robert Lowell, who treated his published work as manuscript, she revised compulsively before letting a poem appear in print, often spending years on a single stanza (or in search of the right *word*), putting it aside and then returning to it again and again. From an early age she admired George Herbert's purity of language, which "manages to express a very deep emotion without straining," and it is the hard-earned purity of her own language that prompted Lowell to see her as an "unerring Muse who makes the casual perfect."

If her luminous body of work seems the product of an unusually serene spirit, this is merely an indication of Elizabeth Bishop's crafty genius. Although a lonely or unhappy childhood is not necessarily conducive to an artistic temperament, it is clear that her own early years introduced her to a lifetime of solitary reading, writing, and dreaming. Born in Worcester, Massachusetts, on February 8, 1911, she was the daughter of William Bishop, a well-to-do builder whose own father started a contracting firm that built the Boston Public Library and the Museum of Fine Arts. Her mother, Gertrude, an emotionally frail woman, was Canadian by birth. William Bishop's death from Bright's disease in his daughter's first year precipitated his wife's collapse, a trauma movingly described in Bishop's most celebrated short story, "In the Village." Gertrude Bishop lived out her life in an insane asylum, and the young girl, virtually orphaned, was sent to live first with her easygoing maternal grandparents in Great Village, Nova Scotia, then with her more formal paternal grandparents in Worcester, and finally with her mother's sister in Boston. Her health was poor—she suffered from severe bronchial colds and asthma—and she spent a good deal of time alone with her books.

After graduating from boarding school in Massachusetts, Bishop attended Vassar, where she started writing and, with her friend Mary McCarthy, helped found a literary magazine. During her senior year she began a friendship with Marianne Moore that she later described in a high-spirited memoir called "Effects of Affection"; their meeting probably influenced her decision not to attend medical school as planned but to become a writer instead.

While still at Vassar she took a three-week walking tour of Newfoundland with a classmate. This excursion marked the beginning of a life of traveling that included time spent in Key West (nearly ten years, during which she painted the appealing watercolors that grace the paperback editions of both *The Complete Poems* and *The Collected Prose*), Europe (France, Spain, Italy, and Ireland), North Africa, and especially Brazil, where she lived during much of her adulthood. One senses that this peripatetic soul, deprived of the security of a permanent childhood home, received as compensation what Ted Morgan calls the instinctive adaptability of the permanently displaced. "Should we have stayed at home, / wherever that may be?" she wonders in "Questions of Travel." Not surprisingly, when asked what she intended to do with the money that came with her Pulitzer prize, she unhesitatingly answered, "Travel." The very titles of her books, not to mention the poems they contain, reveal her passion for gathering experiences from all over the world. "I think geography comes first in my work," she told an interviewer, "and then animals. But I like people too."

North and South, the first of the small volumes she produced over a period of thirty-five years, appeared in 1945. Although her art became richer as she grew older, this early collection, which already reveals a perfect eye for detail, contains several entries to her canon of "engravable" poems, including "The Fish," "The Imaginary Iceberg," "Roosters," and "The Man-Moth." Her second volume, containing nineteen new lyrics, did not appear for nearly a decade, which translates to an average of two poems a year—slow, careful work indeed. Since her new collection was unusually brief and since *North and South* had gone out of print, the two works were combined under the title *A Cold Spring,* which was awarded the Pulitzer Prize. Among the new poems was the enchanting "Invitation to Miss Marianne Moore." In reviewing the book, Lowell wrote that "her tone can be Venetian gorgeous or Quaker simple; she never falls into cant or miserliness," adding that the abundance of description reminds one not of poets ("poor symbolic, abstract creatures") but of the Russian novelists.

In 1951, while traveling in South America, the poet was forced by illness to remain in Brazil for several months, during which time she became captivated by both the country and a remarkable Brazilian woman named Lota de Macedo Soares, who was to be her beloved companion in Rio and in the mountains near Petrópolis for the next fifteen years. In this period of emotional stability, despite being frequently incapacitated by chronic asthma and by alcoholism, with its attendant fits of depression, the permanent tourist produced some fine translations of both poetry and prose, a book-length "history" of the country, and new poems of exceptional beauty inspired by the Brazilian experience. *Questions of Travel* appeared in 1965, and this time Lowell (who visited her in Brazil), impressed by his friend's "tone of large, grave tenderness and sorrowing amusement," observed that when we read Bishop "we enter the classical serenity of a new country."

The Complete Poems (1969), winner of the National Book Award, contains still more work inspired by Brazil, including a lyric set in Ouro Prêto, where the poet restored a colonial house (built in 1690) in a dramatic setting, a home she named Casa Mariana in honor of Marianne Moore. This serene sanctuary, however, was not destined to be a permanent haven. Physical and mental deterioration caused Lota to take her own life during a trip to New York. In 1969 Bishop moved to Boston, living during her last years in a waterfront apartment and, the family inheritance having run out, giving courses at Harvard. She worried throughout her life that revelation of her alcoholism and sexual orientation would affect her reputation and ability to earn a living, but such fears proved groundless. Her final volume, *Geography III,* dedicated to a new companion (and later literary executor), Alice Methfessel, appeared in 1976 and won the National Book Critics Circle award. It contains some of the poet's finest work, including "Crusoe in England," "The Moose," and "One Art." In the same year she became both the first woman and the first American to win the prestigious *Books Abroad*/Neustadt International Prize for Literature.

Elizabeth Bishop died at her home in Boston, in October 1979, of a ruptured cerebral aneurysm. She was sixty-eight and, supported by $21,000 from her second Guggenheim Fellowship (the first was in 1947), was preparing a new collection with the working title "Grandmother's Glass Eye." Although an unbeliever, she was "full of hymns" from her childhood, and in the words of her editor, Robert Giroux, in an introduction to her glorious collected prose, "It was fitting that at her memorial service held at Agassiz House, Harvard, on October 21, 1979, her friends sang 'Rock of Ages,' 'We Gather Together,' 'A Mighty Fortress,' and 'There Is a Balm in Gilead.' "

The Complete Poems: 1927–1979 (Farrar, Straus and Giroux, 1983); *The Collected Prose* (Farrar, Straus and Giroux, 1984); *One Art: elizabeth Bishop Letters,* Selected and Edited by Robert Giroux (Farrar, Straus and Giroux, 1994). Bret C. Milier, *Elizabeth Bishop: Life and the Meaning of It* (University of California Press, 1993). For criticism, see Lorrie Goldensohn, *Elizabeth Bishop: The Biography of a Poetry* (Columbia University Press, 1992); David Kalstone, *Five Temperaments* (Oxford University Press, 1977); *Elizabeth Bishop and Her Art,* edited by Lloyd Schwartz and Sybil P. Estess (University of Michigan Press, 1983).

CHEMIN DE FER

Alone on the railroad track
    I walked with pounding heart.
The ties were too close together
    or maybe too far apart.

The scenery was impoverished:
    scrub-pine and oak; beyond
its mingled gray-green foliage
    I saw the little pond

where the dirty hermit lives,
   lie like an old tear
holding onto its injuries
   lucidly year after year.

The hermit shot off his shot-gun
   and the tree by his cabin shook.
Over the pond went a ripple.
   The pet hen went chook-chook.

"Love should be put into action!"
   screamed the old hermit.
Across the pond an echo
   tried and tried to confirm it.

THE MAN-MOTH*

            Here, above,
cracks in the buildings are filled with battered moonlight.
The whole shadow of Man is only as big as his hat.
It lies at his feet like a circle for a doll to stand on,
and he makes an inverted pin, the point magnetized to the
      moon.
He does not see the moon; he observes only her vast
      properties,
feeling the queer light on his hands, neither warm nor cold,
of a temperature impossible to record in thermometers.

            But when the Man-Moth
pays his rare, although occasional, visits to the surface,
the moon looks rather different to him. He emerges
from an opening under the edge of one of the sidewalks
and nervously begins to scale the faces of the buildings.
He thinks the moon is a small hole at the top of the sky,

*Newspaper misprint for "mammoth."

proving the sky quite useless for protection.
He trembles, but must investigate as high as he can climb.

       Up the façades,
his shadow dragging like a photographer's cloth behind him,
he climbs fearfully, thinking that this time he will manage
to push his small head through that round clean opening
and be forced through, as from a tube, in black scrolls on the
    light.
(Man, standing below him, has no such illusions.)
But what the Man-Moth fears most he must do, although
he fails, of course, and falls back scared but quite unhurt.

       Then he returns
to the pale subways of cement he calls his home. He flits,
he flutters, and cannot get aboard the silent trains
fast enough to suit him. The doors close swiftly.
The Man-Moth always seats himself facing the wrong way
and the train starts at once at its full, terrible speed,
without a shift in gears or a gradation of any sort.
He cannot tell the rate at which he travels backwards.

       Each night he must
be carried through artificial tunnels and dream recurrent
    dreams.
Just as the ties recur beneath his train, these underlie
his rushing brain. He does not dare look out the window,
for the third rail, the unbroken draught of poison,
runs there beside him. He regards it as a disease
he has inherited the susceptibility to. He has to keep
his hands in his pockets, as others must wear mufflers.

       If you catch him,
hold up a flashlight to his eye. It's all dark pupil,
an entire night itself, whose haired horizon tightens
as he stares back, and closes up the eye. Then from the lids
one tear, his only possession, like the bee's sting, slips.

Slyly he palms it, and if you're not paying attention
he'll swallow it. However, if you watch, he'll hand it over,
cool as from underground springs and pure enough to drink.

THE FISH

I caught a tremendous fish
and held him beside the boat
half out of water, with my hook
fast in a corner of his mouth.
He didn't fight.
He hadn't fought at all.
He hung a grunting weight,
battered and venerable
and homely. Here and there
his brown skin hung in strips
like ancient wallpaper,
and its pattern of darker brown
was like wallpaper:
shapes like full-blown roses
stained and lost through age.
He was speckled with barnacles,
fine rosettes of lime,
and infested
with tiny white sea-lice,
and underneath two or three
rags of green weed hung down.
While his gills were breathing in
the terrible oxygen
—the frightening gills,
fresh and crisp with blood,
that can cut so badly—
I thought of the coarse white flesh
packed in like feathers,
the big bones and the little bones,
the dramatic reds and blacks

of his shiny entrails,
and the pink swim-bladder
like a big peony.
I looked into his eyes
which were far larger than mine
but shallower, and yellowed,
the irises backed and packed
with tarnished tinfoil
seen through the lenses
of old scratched isinglass.
They shifted a little, but not
to return my stare.
—It was more like the tipping
of an object toward the light.
I admired his sullen face,
the mechanism of his jaw,
and then I saw
that from his lower lip
—if you could call it a lip—
grim, wet, and weaponlike,
hung five old pieces of fish-line,
or four and a wire leader
with the swivel still attached,
with all their five big hooks
grown firmly in his mouth.
A green line, frayed at the end
where he broke it, two heavier lines,
and a fine black thread
still crimped from the strain and snap
when it broke and he got away.
Like medals with their ribbons
frayed and wavering,
a five-haired beard of wisdom
trailing from his aching jaw.
I stared and stared
and victory filled up
the little rented boat,

from the pool of bilge
where oil had spread a rainbow
around the rusted engine
to the bailer rusted orange,
the sun-cracked thwarts,
the oarlocks on their strings,
the gunnels—until everything
was rainbow, rainbow, rainbow!
And I let the fish go.

AT THE FISHHOUSES

Although it is a cold evening,
down by one of the fishhouses
an old man sits netting,
his net, in the gloaming almost invisible,
a dark purple-brown,
and his shuttle worn and polished.
The air smells so strong of codfish
it makes one's nose run and one's eyes water.
The five fishhouses have steeply peaked roofs
and narrow, cleated gangplanks slant up
to storerooms in the gables
for the wheelbarrows to be pushed up and down on.
All is silver: the heavy surface of the sea,
swelling slowly as if considering spilling over,
is opaque, but the silver of the benches,
the lobster pots, and masts, scattered
among the wild jagged rocks,
is of an apparent translucence
like the small old buildings with an emerald moss
growing on their shoreward walls.
The big fish tubs are completely lined
with layers of beautiful herring scales
and the wheelbarrows are similarly plastered
with creamy iridescent coats of mail,

with small iridescent flies crawling on them.
Up on the little slope behind the houses,
set in the sparse bright sprinkle of grass,
is an ancient wooden capstan,
cracked, with two long bleached handles
and some melancholy stains, like dried blood,
where the ironwork has rusted.
The old man accepts a Lucky Strike.
He was a friend of my grandfather.
We talk of the decline in the population
and of codfish and herring
while he waits for a herring boat to come in.
There are sequins on his vest and on his thumb.
He has scraped the scales, the principal beauty,
from unnumbered fish with that black old knife,
the blade of which is almost worn away.

Down at the water's edge, at the place
where they haul up the boats, up the long ramp
descending into the water, thin silver
tree trunks are laid horizontally
across the gray stones, down and down
at intervals of four or five feet.

Cold dark deep and absolutely clear,
element bearable to no mortal,
to fish and to seals . . . One seal particularly
I have seen here evening after evening.
He was curious about me. He was interested in music;
like me a believer in total immersion,
so I used to sing him Baptist hymns.
I also sang "A Mighty Fortress Is Our God."
He stood up in the water and regarded me
steadily, moving his head a little.
Then he would disappear, then suddenly emerge
almost in the same spot, with a sort of shrug
as if it were against his better judgment.

Cold dark deep and absolutely clear,
the clear gray icy water . . . Back, behind us,
the dignified tall firs begin.
Bluish, associating with their shadows,
a million Christmas trees stand
waiting for Christmas. The water seems suspended
above the rounded gray and blue-gray stones.
I have seen it over and over, the same sea, the same,
slightly, indifferently swinging above the stones,
icily free above the stones,
above the stones and then the world.
If you should dip your hand in,
your wrist would ache immediately,
your bones would begin to ache and your hand would burn
as if the water were a transmutation of fire
that feeds on stones and burns with a dark gray flame.
If you tasted it, it would first taste bitter,
then briny, then surely burn your tongue.
It is like what we imagine knowledge to be:
dark, salt, clear, moving, utterly free,
drawn from the cold hard mouth
of the world, derived from the rocky breasts
forever, flowing and drawn, and since
our knowledge is historical, flowing, and flown.

THE PRODIGAL

The brown enormous odor he lived by
was too close, with its breathing and thick hair,
for him to judge. The floor was rotten; the sty
was plastered halfway up with glass-smooth dung.
Light-lashed, self-righteous, above moving snouts,
the pigs' eyes followed him, a cheerful stare—
even to the sow that always ate her young—
till, sickening, he leaned to scratch her head.
But sometimes mornings after drinking bouts

(he hid the pints behind a two-by-four),
the sunrise glazed the barnyard mud with red;
the burning puddles seemed to reassure.
And then he thought he almost might endure
his exile yet another year or more.

But evenings the first star came to warn.
The farmer whom he worked for came at dark
to shut the cows and horses in the barn
beneath their overhanging clouds of hay,
with pitchforks, faint forked lightnings, catching light,
safe and companionable as in the Ark.
The pigs stuck out their little feet and snored.
The lantern—like the sun, going away—
laid on the mud a pacing aureole.
Carrying a bucket along a slimy board,
he felt the bats' uncertain staggering flight,
his shuddering insights, beyond his control,
touching him. But it took him a long time
finally to make his mind up to go home.

INVITATION TO MISS MARIANNE MOORE

From Brooklyn, over the Brooklyn Bridge, on this fine
     morning,
     please come flying.
In a cloud of fiery pale chemicals,
     please come flying,
to the rapid rolling of thousands of small blue drums
descending out of the mackerel sky
over the glittering grandstand of harbor-water,
     please come flying.

Whistles, pennants and smoke are blowing. The ships
are signaling cordially with multitudes of flags
rising and falling like birds all over the harbor.

Enter: two rivers, gracefully bearing
countless little pellucid jellies
in cut-glass epergnes dragging with silver chains.
The flight is safe; the weather is all arranged.
The waves are running in verses this fine morning.
    Please come flying.

Come with the pointed toe of each black shoe
trailing a sapphire highlight,
with a black capeful of butterfly wings and bon-mots,
with heaven knows how many angels all riding
on the broad black brim of your hat,
    please come flying.

Bearing a musical inaudible abacus,
a slight censorious frown, and blue ribbons,
    please come flying.
Facts and skyscrapers glint in the tide; Manhattan
is all awash with morals this fine morning,
    so please come flying.

Mounting the sky with natural heroism,
above the accidents, above the malignant movies,
the taxicabs and injustices at large,
while horns are resounding in your beautiful ears
that simultaneously listen to
a soft uninvented music, fit for the musk deer,
    please come flying.

For whom the grim museums will behave
like courteous male bower-birds,
for whom the agreeable lions lie in wait
on the steps of the Public Library,
eager to rise and follow through the doors
up into the reading rooms,
    please come flying.
We can sit down and weep; we can go shopping,

or play at a game of constantly being wrong
with a priceless set of vocabularies,
or we can bravely deplore, but please
    please come flying.

With dynasties of negative constructions
darkening and dying around you,
with grammar that suddenly turns and shines
like flocks of sandpipers flying,
    please come flying.

Come like a light in the white mackerel sky,
come like a daytime comet
with a long unnebulous train of words,
from Brooklyn, over the Brooklyn Bridge, on this fine
    morning,
    please come flying.

ARRIVAL AT SANTOS

Here is a coast; here is a harbor;
here, after a meager diet of horizon, is some scenery:
impractically shaped and—who knows?—self-pitying
    mountains,
sad and harsh beneath their frivolous greenery,

with a little church on top of one. And warehouses,
some of them painted a feeble pink, or blue,
and some tall, uncertain palms. Oh, tourist,
is this how this country is going to answer you

and your immodest demands for a different world,
and a better life, and complete comprehension
of both at last, and immediately,
after eighteen days of suspension?

Finish your breakfast. The tender is coming,
a strange and ancient craft, flying a strange and brilliant rag.
So that's the flag. I never saw it before.
I somehow never thought of there *being* a flag,

but of course there was, all along. And coins, I presume,
and paper money; they remain to be seen.
And gingerly now we climb down the ladder backward,
myself and a fellow passenger named Miss Breen,

descending into the midst of twenty-six freighters
waiting to be loaded with green coffee beans.
Please, boy, do be more careful with that boat hook!
Watch out! Oh! It has caught Miss Breen's

skirt! There! Miss Breen is about seventy,
a retired police lieutenant, six feet tall,
with beautiful bright blue eyes and a kind expression.
Her home, when she is at home, is in Glens Fall

s, New York. There. We are settled.
The customs officials will speak English, we hope,
and leave us our bourbon and cigarettes.
Ports are necessities, like postage stamps, or soap,

but they seldom seem to care what impression they make,
or, like this, only attempt, since it does not matter,
the unassertive colors of soap, or postage stamps—
wasting away like the former, slipping the way the latter

do when we mail the letters we wrote on the boat,
either because the glue here is very inferior
or because of the heat. We leave Santos at once;
we are driving to the interior.

THE ARMADILLO

FOR ROBERT LOWELL

This is the time of year
when almost every night
the frail, illegal fire balloons appear.
Climbing the mountain height,

rising toward a saint
still honored in these parts,
the paper chambers flush and fill with light
that comes and goes, like hearts.

Once up against the sky it's hard
to tell them from the stars—
planets, that is—the tinted ones:
Venus going down, or Mars,

or the pale green one. With a wind,
they flare and falter, wobble and toss;
but if it's still they steer between
the kite sticks of the Southern Cross,

receding, dwindling, solemnly
and steadily forsaking us,
or, in the downdraft from a peak,
suddenly turning dangerous.

Last night another big one fell.
It splattered like an egg of fire
against the cliff behind the house.
The flame ran down. We saw the pair

of owls who nest there flying up
and up, their whirling black-and-white
stained bright pink underneath, until
they shrieked up out of sight.

The ancient owls' nest must have burned.
Hastily, all alone,
a glistening armadillo left the scene,
rose-flecked, head down, tail down,

and then a baby rabbit jumped out,
short-eared, to our surprise.
So soft!—a handful of intangible ash
with fixed, ignited eyes.

Too pretty, dreamlike mimicry!
O falling fire and piercing cry
and panic, and a weak mailed fist
clenched ignorant against the sky!

MANNERS

FOR A CHILD OF 1918

My grandfather said to me
as we sat on the wagon seat,
"Be sure to remember to always
speak to everyone you meet."

We met a stranger on foot.
My grandfather's whip tapped his hat.
"Good day, sir. Good day. A fine day."
And I said it and bowed where I sat.

Then we overtook a boy we knew
with his big pet crow on his shoulder.
"Always offer everyone a ride;
don't forget that when you get older,"

my grandfather said. So Willy
climbed up with us, but the crow
gave a "Caw!" and flew off. I was worried.
How would he know where to go?

But he flew a little way at a time
from fence post to fence post, ahead;
and when Willy whistled he answered.
"A fine bird," my grandfather said,

"and he's well brought up. See, he answers
nicely when he's spoken to.
Man or beast, that's good manners.
Be sure that you both always do."

When automobiles went by,
the dust hid the people's faces,
but we shouted "Good day! Good day!
Fine day!" at the top of our voices.

When we came to Hustler Hill,
he said that the mare was tired,
so we all got down and walked,
as our good manners required.

FILLING STATION

Oh, but it is dirty!
—this little filling station,
oil-soaked, oil-permeated
to a disturbing, over-all
black translucency.
Be careful with that match!

Father wears a dirty,
oil-soaked monkey suit
that cuts him under the arms,
and several quick and saucy
and greasy sons assist him
(it's a family filling station),
all quite thoroughly dirty.

Do they live in the station?
It has a cement porch
behind the pumps, and on it
a set of crushed and grease-
impregnated wickerwork;
on the wicker sofa
a dirty dog, quite comfy.

Some comic books provide
the only note of color—
of certain color. They lie
upon a big dim doily
draping a taboret
(part of the set), beside
a big hirsute begonia.

Why the extraneous plant?
Why the taboret?
Why, oh why, the doily?
(Embroidered in daisy stitch
with marguerites, I think,
and heavy with gray crochet.)

Somebody embroidered the doily.
Somebody waters the plant,
or oils it, maybe. Somebody
arranges the rows of cans
so that they softly say:
ESSO—SO—SO—SO
to high-strung automobiles.
Somebody loves us all.

SANDPIPER

The roaring alongside he takes for granted,
and that every so often the world is bound to shake.

He runs, he runs to the south, finical, awkward,
in a state of controlled panic, a student of Blake.

The beach hisses like fat. On his left, a sheet
of interrupting water comes and goes
and glazes over his dark and brittle feet.
He runs, he runs straight through it, watching his toes.

—Watching, rather, the spaces of sand between them,
where (no detail too small) the Atlantic drains
rapidly backwards and downwards. As he runs,
he stares at the dragging grains.

The world is a mist. And then the world is
minute and vast and clear. The tide
is higher or lower. He couldn't tell you which.
His beak is focussed; he is preoccupied,

looking for something, something, something.
Poor bird, he is obsessed!
The millions of grains are black, white, tan, and gray,
mixed with quartz grains, rose and amethyst.

CRUSOE IN ENGLAND

A new volcano has erupted,
the papers say, and last week I was reading
where some ship saw an island being born:
at first a breath of steam, ten miles away;
and then a black fleck—basalt, probably—
rose in the mate's binoculars
and caught on the horizon like a fly.
They named it. But my poor old island's still
un-rediscovered, un-renamable.
None of the books has ever got it right.

Well, I had fifty-two
miserable, small volcanoes I could climb
with a few slithery strides—
volcanoes dead as ash heaps.
I used to sit on the edge of the highest one
and count the others standing up,
naked and leaden, with their heads blown off.
I'd think that if they were the size
I thought volcanoes should be, then I had
become a giant;
and if I had become a giant,
I couldn't bear to think what size
the goats and turtles were,
or the gulls, or the overlapping rollers
—a glittering hexagon of rollers
closing and closing in, but never quite,
glittering and glittering, though the sky
was mostly overcast.

My island seemed to be
a sort of cloud-dump. All the hemisphere's
left-over clouds arrived and hung
above the craters—their parched throats
were hot to touch.
Was that why it rained so much?
And why sometimes the whole place hissed?
The turtles lumbered by, high-domed,
hissing like teakettles.
(And I'd have given years, or taken a few,
for any sort of kettle, of course.)
The folds of lava, running out to sea,
would hiss. I'd turn. And then they'd prove
to be more turtles.
The beaches were all lava, variegated,
black, red, and white, and gray;
the marbled colors made a fine display.
And I had waterspouts. Oh,

half a dozen at a time, far out,
they'd come and go, advancing and retreating,
their heads in cloud, their feet in moving patches
of scuffed-up white.
Glass chimneys, flexible, attenuated,
sacerdotal beings of glass . . . I watched
the water spiral up in them like smoke.
Beautiful, yes, but not much company.

I often gave way to self-pity.
"Do I deserve this? I suppose I must.
I wouldn't be here otherwise. Was there
a moment when I actually chose this?
I don't remember, but there could have been."
What's wrong about self-pity, anyway?
With my legs dangling down familiarly
over a crater's edge, I told myself
"Pity should begin at home." So the more
pity I felt, the more I felt at home.

The sun set in the sea; the same odd sun
rose from the sea,
and there was one of it and one of me.
The island had one kind of everything:
one tree snail, a bright violet-blue
with a thin shell, crept over everything,
over the one variety of tree,
a sooty, scrub affair.
Snail shells lay under these in drifts
and, at a distance,
you'd swear that they were beds of irises.
There was one kind of berry, a dark red.
I tried it, one by one, and hours apart.
Sub-acid, and not bad, no ill effects;
and so I made home-brew. I'd drink
the awful, fizzy, stinging stuff
that went straight to my head

and play my home-made flute
(I think it had the weirdest scale on earth)
and, dizzy, whoop and dance among the goats.
Home-made, home-made! But aren't we all?
I felt a deep affection for
the smallest of my island industries.
No, not exactly, since the smallest was
a miserable philosophy.

Because I didn't know enough.
Why didn't I know enough of something?
Greek drama or astronomy? The books
I'd read were full of blanks;
the poems—well, I tried
reciting to my iris-beds,
"They flash upon that inward eye,
which is the bliss . . ." The bliss of what?
One of the first things that I did
when I got back was look it up.

The island smelled of goat and guano.
The goats were white, so were the gulls,
and both too tame, or else they thought
I was a goat, too, or a gull.
Baa, baa, baa and *shriek, shriek, shriek,*
baa . . . shriek . . . baa . . . I still can't shake
them from my ears; they're hurting now.
The questioning shrieks, the equivocal replies
over a ground of hissing rain
and hissing, ambulating turtles
got on my nerves.
When all the gulls flew up at once, they sounded
like a big tree in a strong wind, its leaves.
I'd shut my eyes and think about a tree,
an oak, say, with real shade, somewhere.
I'd heard of cattle getting island-sick.

I thought the goats were.
One billy-goat would stand on the volcano
I'd christened *Mont d'Espoir* or *Mount Despair*
(I'd time enough to play with names),
and bleat and bleat, and sniff the air.
I'd grab his beard and look at him.
His pupils, horizontal, narrowed up
and expressed nothing, or a little malice.
I got so tired of the very colors!
One day I dyed a baby goat bright red
with my red berries, just to see
something a little different.
And then his mother wouldn't recognize him.

Dreams were the worst. Of course I dreamed of food
and love, but they were pleasant rather
than otherwise. But then I'd dream of things
like slitting a baby's throat, mistaking it
for a baby goat. I'd have
nightmares of other islands
stretching away from mine, infinities
of islands, islands spawning islands,
like frogs' eggs turning into polliwogs
of islands, knowing that I had to live
on each and every one, eventually,
for ages, registering their flora,
their fauna, their geography.

Just when I thought I couldn't stand it
another minute longer, Friday came.
(Accounts of that have everything all wrong.)
Friday was nice.
Friday was nice, and we were friends.
If only he had been a woman!
I wanted to propagate my kind,
and so did he, I think, poor boy.

He'd pet the baby goats sometimes,
and race with them, or carry one around.
—Pretty to watch; he had a pretty body.

And then one day they came and took us off.

Now I live here, another island,
that doesn't seem like one, but who decides?
My blood was full of them; my brain
bred islands. But that archipelago
has petered out. I'm old.
I'm bored, too, drinking my real tea,
surrounded by uninteresting lumber.
The knife there on the shelf—
it reeked of meaning, like a crucifix.
It lived. How many years did I
beg it, implore it, not to break?
I knew each nick and scratch by heart,
the bluish blade, the broken tip,
the lines of wood-grain on the handle . . .
Now it won't look at me at all.
The living soul has dribbled away.
My eyes rest on it and pass on.

The local museum's asked me to
leave everything to them:
the flute, the knife, the shrivelled shoes,
my shedding goatskin trousers
(moths have got in the fur),
the parasol that took me such a time
remembering the way the ribs should go.
It still will work but, folded up,
looks like a plucked and skinny fowl.
How can anyone want such things?
—And Friday, my dear Friday, died of measles
seventeen years ago come March.

THE MOOSE

FOR GRACE BULMER BOWERS

From narrow provinces
of fish and bread and tea,
home of the long tides
where the bay leaves the sea
twice a day and takes
the herrings long rides,

where if the river
enters or retreats
in a wall of brown foam
depends on if it meets
the bay coming in,
the bay not at home;

where, silted red,
sometimes the sun sets
facing a red sea,
and others, veins the flats'
lavender, rich mud
in burning rivulets;

on red, gravelly roads,
down rows of sugar maples,
past clapboard farmhouses
and neat, clapboard churches,
bleached, ridged as clamshells,
past twin silver birches,

through late afternoon
a bus journeys west,
the windshield flashing pink,
pink glancing off of metal,
brushing the dented flank
of blue, beat-up enamel;

down hollows, up rises,
and waits, patient, while
a lone traveller gives
kisses and embraces
to seven relatives
and a collie supervises.

Goodbye to the elms,
to the farm, to the dog.
The bus starts. The light
grows richer; the fog,
shifting, salty, thin,
comes closing in.

Its cold, round crystals
form and slide and settle
in the white hens' feathers,
in gray glazed cabbages,
on the cabbage roses
and lupins like apostles;

the sweet peas cling
to their wet white string
on the whitewashed fences;
bumblebees creep
inside the foxgloves,
and evening commences.

One stop at Bass River.
Then the Economies—
Lower, Middle, Upper;
Five Islands, Five Houses,
where a woman shakes a tablecloth
out after supper.

A pale flickering. Gone.
The Tantramar marshes

and the smell of salt hay.
An iron bridge trembles
and a loose plank rattles
but doesn't give way.

On the left, a red light
swims through the dark:
a ship's port lantern.
Two rubber boots show,
illuminated, solemn.
A dog gives one bark.

A woman climbs in
with two market bags,
brisk, freckled, elderly.
"A grand night. Yes, sir,
all the way to Boston."
She regards us amicably.

Moonlight as we enter
the New Brunswick woods,
hairy, scratchy, splintery;
moonlight and mist
caught in them like lamb's wool
on bushes in a pasture.

The passengers lie back.
Snores. Some long sighs.
A dreamy divagation
begins in the night,
a gentle, auditory,
slow hallucination. . . .

In the creakings and noises,
an old conversation
—not concerning us,
but recognizable, somewhere,

back in the bus:
Grandparents' voices

uninterruptedly
talking, in Eternity:
names being mentioned,
things cleared up finally;
what he said, what she said,
who got pensioned;

deaths, deaths and sicknesses;
the year he remarried;
the year (something) happened.
She died in childbirth.
That was the son lost
when the schooner foundered.

He took to drink. Yes.
She went to the bad.
When Amos began to pray
even in the store and
finally the family had
to put him away.

"Yes . . . " that peculiar
affirmative. "Yes . . . "
A sharp, indrawn breath,
half groan, half acceptance,
that means "Life's like that.
We know *it* (also death)."

Talking the way they talked
in the old featherbed,
peacefully, on and on,
dim lamplight in the hall,
down in the kitchen, the dog
tucked in her shawl.

Now, it's all right now
even to fall asleep
just as on all those nights.
—Suddenly the bus driver
stops with a jolt,
turns off his lights.

A moose has come out of
the impenetrable wood
and stands there, looms, rather,
in the middle of the road.
It approaches; it sniffs at
the bus's hot hood.

Towering, antlerless,
high as a church,
homely as a house
(or, safe as houses).
A man's voice assures us
"Perfectly harmless. . . . "

Some of the passengers
exclaim in whispers,
childishly, softly,
"Sure are big creatures."
"It's awful plain."
"Look! It's a she!"

Taking her time,
she looks the bus over,
grand, otherworldly.
Why, why do we feel
(we all feel) this sweet
sensation of joy?

"Curious creatures,"
says our quiet driver,

rolling his *r*'s.
"Look at that, would you."
Then he shifts gears.
For a moment longer,

by craning backward,
the moose can be seen
on the moonlit macadam;
then there's a dim
smell of moose, an acrid
smell of gasoline.

ONE ART

The art of losing isn't hard to master;
so many things seem filled with the intent
to be lost that their loss is no disaster.

Lose something every day. Accept the fluster
of lost door keys, the hour badly spent.
The art of losing isn't hard to master.

Then practice losing farther, losing faster:
places, and names, and where it was you meant
to travel. None of these will bring disaster.

I lost my mother's watch. And look! my last, or
next-to-last, of three loved houses went.
The art of losing isn't hard to master.

I lost two cities, lovely ones. And, vaster,
some realms I owned, two rivers, a continent.
I miss them, but it wasn't a disaster.

—Even losing you (the joking voice, a gesture
I love) I shan't have lied. It's evident

the art of losing's not too hard to master
though it may look like (*Write* it!) like disaster.

PINK DOG

[RIO DE JANEIRO]

The sun is blazing and the sky is blue.
Umbrellas clothe the beach in every hue.
Naked, you trot across the avenue.

Oh, never have I seen a dog so bare!
Naked and pink, without a single hair . . .
Startled, the passersby draw back and stare.

Of course they're mortally afraid of rabies.
You are not mad; you have a case of scabies
but look intelligent. Where are your babies?

(A nursing mother, by those hanging teats.)
In what slum have you hidden them, poor bitch,
while you go begging, living by your wits?

Didn't you know? It's been in all the papers,
to solve this problem, how they deal with beggars?
They take and throw them in the tidal rivers.

Yes, idiots, paralytics, parasites
go bobbing in the ebbing sewage, nights
out in the suburbs, where there are no lights.

If they do this to anyone who begs,
drugged, drunk, or sober, with or without legs,
what would they do to sick, four-leggèd dogs?

In the cafés and on the sidewalk corners
the joke is going round that all the beggars
who can afford them now wear life preservers.

In your condition you would not be able
even to float, much less to dog-paddle.
Now look, the practical, the sensible

solution is to wear a *fantasía*.★
Tonight you simply can't afford to be a-
n eyesore. But no one will ever see a

dog in *máscara* this time of year.
Ash Wednesday'll come but Carnival is here.
What sambas can you dance? What will you wear?

They say that Carnival's degenerating
—radios, Americans, or something,
have ruined it completely. They're just talking.

Carnival is always wonderful!
A depilated dog would not look well.
Dress up! Dress up and dance at Carnival!

LULLABY FOR THE CAT

Minnow, go to sleep and dream,
　　Close your great big eyes;
Round your bed Events prepare
　　The pleasantest surprise.

Darling Minnow, drop that frown,
　　Just cooperate,
Not a kitten shall be drowned
　　In the Marxist State.

Joy and Love will both be yours,
　　Minnow, don't be glum.
Happy days are coming soon—
　　Sleep, and let them come . . .

★*Carnival costume.*

ROBERT LOWELL

after. His behavior preceding and during his manic periods was characterized by delusions of grandeur, identification with notorious historical figures, and, on occasion, by physical violence, sometimes requiring restraint by force and heavy sedation. Nevertheless, he was able, in poems like "Waking in the Blue" and "Man and Wife," to transmute his soul's nightmares into art of dark beauty. Toward the end of his life, following the discovery of lithium carbonate, he expressed a painful realization to Robert Giroux: "It's terrible, Bob, to think that all I've suffered, and all the suffering I've caused, might have arisen from the lack of a little salt in my brain."

Unlike most American poets, who are known, if at all, only to their fellow writers and, if they are lucky, to a small audience of admirers, Lowell was always a highly visible figure, probably—with the possible exceptions of Norman Mailer and Allen Ginsberg—the most publicized writer of his time. He was, in Peter Conn's words, "the resisting heir of ten generations of New England achievement," and his career, as a result, involved a notable pattern of repudiations. Coming as he did from a long line of New England Episcopalians, he attracted attention when, before his first marriage, he converted to Catholicism, "the church of Boston immigrants," and became, at least for several years, a decidedly religious poet, drawing on ecclesiastical imagery. The title of his first book, *Land of Unlikeness,* comes from Etienne Gilson's observation in *The Mystical Theology of Saint Bernard* that a godless soul inhabits a "land of unlikeness." He later abandoned Christian symbols, having become "a slavish convert" to Freud: "My dreams," he wrote, "are more rewarding than my actuality." After 1950, in David Perkins's words, "God no longer existed in Lowell's universe, though he sometimes mentioned Him unfavorably."

When, appalled by the bombing of civilians, he declared himself a conscientious objector in 1943 (and spent six months in jail as "a fire-breathing Catholic C. O."), *The New York Times* carried a story with the headline A BOSTON LOWELL IS A DRAFT DODGER. And when, in 1965, in the midst of the Vietnam War, he refused an invitation to a White House Festival of the Arts, his letter to President Johnson was printed on the front page of the *Times*. His participation in an anti–Vietnam War march on the Pentagon in 1964 also received a good deal of comment, most significantly in Mailer's *Armies of the Night,* which contains one of the more perceptive (albeit somewhat hostile) descriptions we have of the poet, with his "unwilling haunted saintliness," and "fine stammering voice which gave the impression that life rushed at him like a series of hurdles and some he succeeded in jumping and some he did not."

Like others represented in this book, especially Elizabeth Bishop and James Merrill, Lowell is a consummate craftsman—a master of forms, musical effects, rhymes and off-rhymes—who is able to transform his transient experience into timeless artifacts. "Taste the phrases," Sylvia Plath exclaimed in her journal, finding them "tough, knotty, blazing with color and fury, most eminently sayable." Blessed with a flawless ear, he is able to make the English language do fresh and unexpected things in ways that seem effortless even when he is re-creating his traumatic emotional descents. "You can say anything in a poem," he declared, "if you *place* it properly." This is impressive evidence of an art that conceals art, that creates an impression of inevitability when in fact every syllable has been patted into place, or, through endless revision, scrupulously replaced. Nothing is left to chance, but it all seems somehow preordained. Especially in the later work, the hard-earned directness conceals a good deal of structural sophistication; repeated readings invariably yield unsuspected complexities.

The work is learned and wide-ranging. Save for a consistent preoccupation with history (Richard Poirier calls him "our truest historian"), a powerful sense of landscape, a tendency to become didactic, and a fusion of personal concerns with social issues, there is a good deal of variety from book to book. All his critics comment on a dramatic shift from the insistent symbolism and allusive rhetoric of the first three—*Land of Unlikeness* (1944), *Lord Weary's Castle* (1946), and *The Mills of the Kavanaughs* (1951)—to the more accessible, informal, even prosaic language of *Life Studies,* composed after Lowell heard Ginsberg read from

Howl, an experience that convinced him of the unnecessary obscurity of his own work.

He continued to present himself with less ambiguity and literary artifice in such later volumes as *For the Union Dead* (1964); *Near the Ocean* (1967); *The Dolphin,* awarded a Pulitzer Prize in 1964; and *Day by Day,* which won the National Book Critics Award in 1977, the year he died of heart failure. Even when his poems seem most free, however, subtle patterns invariably join the typically immense number of observed details into an artistically cohesive whole. His remarkable sensitivity to the nuances of language are also evident in his translations of Racine's *Phaedra* and Aeschylus's *Oresteia* as well as in his powerful dramatizations of stories by Hawthorne and Melville, called *The Old Glory,* which were performed to considerable acclaim off-Broadway in 1964.

If Lowell's technical repertoire is varied, so too are his subjects, though I am increasingly won over by John Unterecker's observation that all the poems, however different in style and subject matter, finally cohere into a vast single work, "the record of an 'I' who emerges out of literature, history, and autobiography into the jumble of other lived lives." The poet himself referred to his books as "my autobiography in verse." I agree, too, with Mark Rudman's assertion that Lowell could "salvage the most intractable material, like an archaeologist," consistently finding significance in the most poetically unpromising places. In addition to his obsessive reading, the source of his striking allusiveness, Lowell was also an obsessive reviser, unable to look at one of his poems without making changes. (One thinks of Bonnard, who was once arrested in the Paris Museum of Modern Art for touching up his own pastels on display there.) Lowell could never stop rewriting, handling even his published work "as if it were manuscript," he said at one point. What he offers us, as a result, in Ian Hamilton's words, are "a series of possible drafts."

Since his troubled spirit is now at rest, there will be no further fine-tunings of his poetry, as intelligent and polished a body of work as any American poet has produced. There are those who maintained, following the deaths of Stevens, Frost, Williams, Moore, and Eliot, that there were no longer any giants among us. Lowell's "possible drafts," as I hope those I have selected make clear, suggest otherwise.

Selected Poems, revised edition (Farrar, Straus and Giroux, 1977); *Collected Prose* (Farrar, Straus and Giroux, 1987). Ian Hamilton, *Robert Lowell: A Biography* (Random House, 1982). For criticism see Vereen M. Bell, *Robert Lowell: Nihilist as Hero* (Harvard University Press, 1982), and Mark Rudman, *Robert Lowell: An Introduction to the Poetry* (Columbia University Press, 1983).

THE QUAKER GRAVEYARD IN NANTUCKET

[FOR WARREN WINSLOW, DEAD AT SEA]

Let man have dominion over the fishes of the sea and the fowls of the air and the beasts of the whole earth, and every creeping creature that moveth upon the earth.

I

A brackish reach of shoal off Madaket—
The sea was still breaking violently and night
Had steamed into our North Atlantic Fleet,
When the drowned sailor clutched the drag-net. Light
Flashed from his matted head and marble feet,
He grappled at the net
With the coiled, hurdling muscles of his thighs:
The corpse was bloodless, a botch of reds and whites,
Its open, staring eyes
Were lustreless dead-lights
Or cabin-windows on a stranded hulk
Heavy with sand. We weight the body, close
Its eyes and heave it seaward whence it came,
Where the heel-headed dogfish barks its nose

On Ahab's void and forehead; and the name
Is blocked in yellow chalk.
Sailors, who pitch this portent at the sea
Where dreadnaughts shall confess
Its hell-bent deity,
When you are powerless
To sand-bag this Atlantic bulwark, faced
By the earth-shaker, green, unwearied, chaste
In his steel scales: ask for no Orphean lute
To pluck life back. The guns of the steeled fleet
Recoil and then repeat
The hoarse salute.

II

Whenever winds are moving and their breath
Heaves at the roped-in bulwarks of this pier,
The terns and sea-gulls tremble at your death
In these home waters. Sailor, can you hear
The Pequod's sea wings, beating landward, fall
Headlong and break on our Atlantic wall
Off 'Sconset, where the yawing S-boats splash
The bellbuoy, with ballooning spinnakers,
As the entangled, screeching mainsheet clears
The blocks: off Madaket, where lubbers lash
The heavy surf and throw their long lead squids
For blue-fish? Sea-gulls blink their heavy lids
Seaward. The winds' wings beat upon the stones,
Cousin, and scream for you and the claws rush
At the sea's throat and wring it in the slush
Of this old Quaker graveyard where the bones
Cry out in the long night for the hurt beast
Bobbing by Ahab's whaleboats in the East.

III

All you recovered from Poseidon died
With you, my cousin, and the harrowed brine
Is fruitless on the blue beard of the god,

Stretching beyond us to the castles in Spain,
Nantucket's westward haven. To Cape Cod
Guns, cradled on the tide,
Blast the eelgrass about a waterclock
Of bilge and backwash, roil the salt and sand
Lashing earth's scaffold, rock
Our warships in the hand
Of the great God, where time's contrition blues
Whatever it was these Quaker sailors lost
In the mad scramble of their lives. They died
When time was open-eyed,
Wooden and childish; only bones abide
There, in the nowhere, where their boats were tossed
Sky-high, where mariners had fabled news
Of IS, the whited monster. What it cost
Them is their secret. In the sperm-whale's slick
I see the Quakers drown and hear their cry:
"If God himself had not been on our side,
If God himself had not been on our side,
When the Atlantic rose against us, why,
Then it had swallowed us up quick."

IV

This is the end of the whaleroad and the whale
Who spewed Nantucket bones on the thrashed swell
And stirred the troubled waters to whirlpools
To send the Pequod packing off to hell:
This is the end of them, three-quarters fools,
Snatching at straws to sail
Seaward and seaward on the turntail whale,
Spouting out blood and water as it rolls,
Sick as a dog to these Atlantic shoals:
Clamavimus, O depths. Let the sea-gulls wail

For water, for the deep where the high tide
Mutters to its hurt self, mutters and ebbs.
Waves wallow in their wash, go out and out,

Leave only the death-rattle of the crabs,
The beach increasing, its enormous snout
Sucking the ocean's side.
This is the end of running on the waves;
We are poured out like water. Who will dance
The mast-lashed master of Leviathans
Up from this field of Quakers in their unstoned graves?

V

When the whale's viscera go and the roll
Of its corruption overruns this world
Beyond tree-swept Nantucket and Woods Hole
And Martha's Vineyard, Sailor, will your sword
Whistle and fall and sink into the fat?
In the great ash-pit of Jehoshaphat
The bones cry for the blood of the white whale,
The fat flukes arch and whack about its ears,
The death-lance churns into the sanctuary, tears
The gun-blue swingle, heaving like a flail,
And hacks the coiling life out: it works and drags
And rips the sperm-whale's midriff into rags,
Gobbets of blubber spill to wind and weather,
Sailor, and gulls go round the stoven timbers
Where the morning stars sing out together
And thunder shakes the white surf and dismembers
The red flag hammered in the mast-head. Hide,
Our steel, Jonas Messias, in Thy side.

VI

OUR LADY OF WALSINGHAM

There once the penitents took off their shoes
And then walked barefoot the remaining mile;
And the small trees, a stream and hedgerows file
Slowly along the munching English lane,
Like cows to the old shrine, until you lose
Track of your dragging pain.

The stream flows down under the druid tree,
Shiloah's whirlpools gurgle and make glad
The castle of God. Sailor, you were glad
And whistled Sion by that stream. But see:

Our Lady, too small for her canopy,
Sits near the altar. There's no comeliness
At all or charm in that expressionless
Face with its heavy eyelids. As before,
This face, for centuries a memory,
Non est species, neque decor,
Expressionless, expresses God: it goes
Past castled Sion. She knows what God knows,
Not Calvary's Cross nor crib at Bethlehem
Now, and the world shall come to Walsingham.

VII

The empty winds are creaking and the oak
Splatters and splatters on the cenotaph,
The boughs are trembling and a gaff
Bobs on the untimely stroke
Of the greased wash exploding on a shoal-bell
In the old mouth of the Atlantic. It's well;
Atlantic, you are fouled with the blue sailors,
Sea-monsters, upward angel, downward fish:
Unmarried and corroding, spare of flesh
Mart once of supercilious, wing'd clippers,
Atlantic, where your bell-trap guts its spoil
You could cut the brackish winds with a knife
Here in Nantucket, and cast up the time
When the Lord God formed man from the sea's slime
And breathed into his face the breath of life,
And blue-lung'd combers lumbered to the kill.
The Lord survives the rainbow of His will.

MARY WINSLOW

Her Irish maids could never spoon out mush
Or orange-juice enough; the body cools
And smiles as a sick child
Who adds up figures, and a hush
Grips at the poised relations sipping sherry
And tracking up the carpets of her four
Room kingdom. On the rigid Charles, in snow,
Charon, the Lubber, clambers from his wherry,
And stops her hideous baby-squawks and yells,
Wit's clownish afterthought. Nothing will go
Again. Even the gelded picador
Baiting the twinned runt bulls
With walrus horns before the Spanish Belles
Is veiled with all the childish bibelots.

Mary Winslow is dead. Out on the Charles
The shells hold water and their oarblades drag,
Littered with captivated ducks, and now
The bell-rope in King's Chapel Tower unsnarls
And bells the bestial cow
From Boston Common; she is dead. But stop,
Neighbor, these pillows prop
Her that her terrified and child's cold eyes
Glass what they're not: our Copley ancestress,
Grandiloquent, square-jowled and worldly-wise,
A Cleopatra in her housewife's dress;
Nothing will go again. The bells cry: "Come,
Come home," the babbling Chapel belfry cries:
"Come, Mary Winslow, come; I bell thee home."

AFTER THE SURPRISING CONVERSIONS

September twenty-second, Sir: today
I answer. In the latter part of May,
Hard on our Lord's Ascension, it began
To be more sensible. A gentleman
Of more than common understanding, strict
In morals, pious in behavior, kicked
Against our goad. A man of some renown,
An useful, honored person in the town,
He came of melancholy parents; prone
To secret spells, for years they kept alone—
His uncle, I believe, was killed of it:
Good people, but of too much or little wit.
I preached one Sabbath on a text from Kings;
He showed concernment for his soul. Some things
In his experience were hopeful. He
Would sit and watch the wind knocking a tree
And praise this countryside our Lord has made.
Once when a poor man's heifer died, he laid
A shilling on the doorsill; though a thirst
For loving shook him like a snake, he durst
Not entertain much hope of his estate
In heaven. Once we saw him sitting late
Behind his attic window by a light
That guttered on his Bible; through that night
He meditated terror, and he seemed
Beyond advice or reason, for he dreamed
That he was called to trumpet Judgment Day
To Concord. In the latter part of May
He cut his throat. And though the coroner
Judged him delirious, soon a noisome stir
Palsied our village. At Jehovah's nod
Satan seemed more let loose amongst us: God
Abandoned us to Satan, and he pressed
Us hard, until we thought we could not rest

Till we had done with life. Content was gone.
All the good work was quashed. We were undone.
The breath of God had carried out a planned
And sensible withdrawal from this land;
The multitude, once unconcerned with doubt,
Once neither callous, curious nor devout,
Jumped at broad noon, as though some peddler groaned
At it in its familiar twang: "My friend,
Cut your own throat. Cut your own throat. Now! Now!"
September twenty-second, Sir, the bough
Cracks with the unpicked apples, and at dawn
The small-mouth bass breaks water, gorged with spawn.

To Delmore Schwartz

(Cambridge 1946)

We couldn't even keep the furnace lit!
Even when we had disconnected it,
the antiquated
refrigerator gurgled mustard gas
through your mustard-yellow house,
and spoiled our long maneuvered visit
from T. S. Eliot's brother, Henry Ware. . . .

Your stuffed duck craned toward Harvard from my trunk:
its bill was a black whistle, and its brow
was high and thinner than a baby's thumb;
its webs were tough as toenails on its bough.
It was your first kill; you had rushed it home,
pickled in a tin wastebasket of rum—
it looked through us, as if it'd died dead drunk.
You must have propped its eyelids with a nail,
and yet it lived with us and met our stare,
Rabelaisian, lubricious, drugged. And there,
perched on my trunk and typing-table,
it cooled our universal

Angst a moment, Delmore. We drank and eyed
the chicken-hearted shadows of the world.
Underseas fellows, nobly mad,
we talked away our friends. "Let Joyce and Freud,
the Masters of Joy,
be our guests here," you said. The room was filled
with cigarette smoke circling the paranoid,
inert gaze of Coleridge, back
from Malta—his eyes lost in flesh, lips baked and black.
Your tiger kitten, *Oranges,*
cartwheeled for joy in a ball of snarls.
You said:
"We poets in our youth begin in sadness;
thereof in the end come despondency and madness;
Stalin has had two cerebral hemorrhages!"
The Charles
River was turning silver. In the ebb-
light of morning, we stuck
the duck
-'s web-
foot, like a candle, in a quart of gin we'd killed.

My Last Afternoon
with Uncle Devereux Winslow

1922: the stone porch of my Grandfather's summer house

I

"I won't go with you. I want to stay with Grandpa!"
That's how I threw cold water
on my Mother and Father's
watery martini pipe dreams at Sunday dinner.
. . . Fontainebleau, Mattapoisett, Puget Sound. . . .
Nowhere was anywhere after a summer
at my Grandfather's farm.

Diamond-pointed, athirst and Norman,
its alley of poplars
paraded from Grandmother's rose garden
to a scary stand of virgin pine,
scrub, and paths forever pioneering.

One afternoon in 1922,
I sat on the stone porch, looking through
screens as black-grained as drifting coal.
Tockytock, tockytock
clumped our Alpine, Edwardian cuckoo clock,
slung with strangled, wooden game.
Our farmer was cementing a root-house under the hill.
One of my hands was cool on a pile
of black earth, the other warm
on a pile of lime. All about me
were the works of my Grandfather's hands:
snapshots of his *Liberty Bell* silver mine;
his high school at *Stuttgart am Neckar;*
stogie-brown beams; fools'-gold nuggets;
octagonal red tiles,
sweaty with a secret dank, crummy with ant-stale;
a Rocky Mountain chaise longue,
its legs, shellacked saplings.
A pastel-pale Huckleberry Finn
fished with a broom straw in a basin
hollowed out of a millstone.
Like my Grandfather, the décor
was manly, comfortable,
overbearing, disproportioned.

What were those sunflowers? Pumpkins floating
     shoulder-high?
It was sunset, Sadie and Nellie
bearing pitchers of ice-tea,
oranges, lemons, mint, and peppermints,
and the jug of shandygaff,

which Grandpa made by blending half and half
yeasty, wheezing homemade sarsaparilla with beer.
The farm, entitled *Char-de-sa*
in the Social Register,
was named for my Grandfather's children:
Charlotte, Devereux, and Sarah.
No one had died there in my lifetime . . .
Only Cinder, our Scottie puppy
paralyzed from gobbling toads.
I sat mixing black earth and lime.

II

I was five and a half.
My formal pearl gray shorts
had been worn for three minutes.
My perfection was the Olympian
poise of my models in the imperishable autumn
display windows
of Rogers Peet's boys' store below the State House
in Boston. Distorting drops of water
pinpricked my face in the basin's mirror.
I was a stuffed toucan
with a bibulous, multicolored beak.

III

Up in the air
by the lakeview window in the billiards-room,
lurid in the doldrums of the sunset hour,
my Great Aunt Sarah
was learning *Samson and Delilah*.
She thundered on the keyboard of her dummy piano,
with gauze curtains like a boudoir table,
accordionlike yet soundless.
It had been bought to spare the nerves
of my Grandmother,
tone-deaf, quick as a cricket,
now needing a fourth for "Auction,"

and casting a thirsty eye
on Aunt Sarah, risen like the phoenix
from her bed of troublesome snacks and Tauchnitz classics.

Forty years earlier,
twenty, auburn headed,
grasshopper notes of genius!
Family gossip says Aunt Sarah
tilted her archaic Athenian nose
and jilted an Astor.
Each morning she practiced
on the grand piano at Symphony Hall,
deathlike in the off-season summer—
its naked Greek statues draped with purple
like the saints in Holy Week. . . .
On the recital day, she failed to appear.

IV

I picked with a clean finger nail at the blue anchor
on my sailor blouse washed white as a spinnaker.
What in the world was I wishing?
. . . A sail-colored horse browsing in the bullrushes . . .
A fluff of the west wind puffing
my blouse, kiting me over our seven chimneys,
troubling the waters. . . .
As small as sapphires were the ponds: *Quittacus, Snippituit,*
and *Assawompset,* halved by "the Island,"
where my Uncle's duck blind
floated in a barrage of smoke-clouds.
Double-barreled shotguns
stuck out like bundles of baby crow-bars.
A single sculler in a camouflaged kayak
was quacking to the decoys. . . .

At the cabin between the waters,
the nearest windows were already boarded.
Uncle Devereux was closing camp for the winter.

As if posed for "the engagement photograph,"
he was wearing his severe
war-uniform of a volunteer Canadian officer.
Daylight from the doorway riddled his student posters,
tacked helter-skelter on walls as raw as a boardwalk.
Mr. Punch, a water melon in hockey tights,
was tossing off a decanter of Scotch.
La Belle France in a red, white and blue toga
was accepting the arm of her "protector,"
the ingenu and porcine Edward VII.
The pre-war music hall belles
had goose necks, glorious signatures, beauty-moles,
and coils of hair like rooster tails.
The finest poster was two or three young men in khaki kilts
being bushwhacked on the veldt—
They were almost life-size. . . .

My Uncle was dying at twenty-nine.
"You are behaving like children,"
said my Grandfather,
when my Uncle and Aunt left their three baby daughters,
and sailed for Europe on a last honeymoon . . .
I cowered in terror.
I wasn't a child at all—
unseen and all-seeing, I was Agrippina
in the Golden House of Nero. . . .
Near me was the white measuring-door
my Grandfather had penciled with my Uncle's heights.
In 1911, he had stopped growing at just six feet.
While I sat on the tiles,
and dug at the anchor on my sailor blouse,
Uncle Devereux stood behind me.
He was as brushed as Bayard, our riding horse.
His face was putty.
His blue coat and white trousers
grew sharper and straighter.
His coat was a blue jay's tail,

his trousers were solid cream from the top of the bottle.
He was animated, hierarchical,
like a ginger snap man in a clothes-press.
He was dying of the incurable Hodgkin's disease. . . .
My hands were warm, then cool, on the piles
of earth and lime,
a black pile and a white pile. . . .
Come winter,
Uncle Devereux would blend to the one color.

TERMINAL DAYS AT BEVERLY FARMS

At Beverly Farms, a portly, uncomfortable boulder
bulked in the garden's center—
an irregular Japanese touch.
After his Bourbon "old fashioned," Father,
bronzed, breezy, a shade too ruddy,
swayed as if on deck duty
under his six pointed star-lantern—
last July's birthday present.
He smiled his oval Lowell smile,
he wore his cream gabardine dinner-jacket,
and indigo cummerbund.
His head was efficient and hairless,
his newly dieted figure was vitally trim.

Father and Mother moved to Beverly Farms
to be a two-minute walk from the station,
half an hour by train from the Boston doctors.
They had no sea-view,
but sky-blue tracks of the commuters' railroad shone
like a double-barreled shotgun
through the scarlet late August sumac,
multiplying like cancer
at their garden's border.

Father had had two coronaries.
He still treasured underhand economies,
but his best friend was his little black Chevy,
garaged like a sacrificial steer
with gilded hooves,
yet sensationally sober,
and with less side than an old dancing pump.
The local dealer, a "buccaneer,"
had been bribed a "king's ransom"
to quickly deliver a car without chrome.

Each morning at eight-thirty,
inattentive and beaming,
loaded with his "calc" and "trig" books,
his clipper ship statistics,
and his ivory slide rule,
Father stole off with the Chevy
to loaf in the Maritime Museum at Salem.
He called the curator
"the commander of the Swiss Navy."

Father's death was abrupt and unprotesting.
His vision was still twenty-twenty.
After a morning of anxious, repetitive smiling,
his last words to Mother were:
"I feel awful."

WAKING IN THE BLUE

The night attendant, a B.U. sophomore,
rouses from the mare's-nest of his drowsy head
propped on *The Meaning of Meaning*.
He catwalks down our corridor.
Azure day
makes my agonized blue window bleaker.
Crows maunder on the petrified fairway.

Absence! My heart grows tense
as though a harpoon were sparring for the kill.
(This is the house for the "mentally ill.")

What use is my sense of humor?
I grin at Stanley, now sunk in his sixties,
once a Harvard all-American fullback
(if such were possible!),
still hoarding the build of a boy in his twenties,
as he soaks, a ramrod
with the muscle of a seal
in his long tub,
vaguely urinous from the Victorian plumbing.
A kingly granite profile in a crimson golf cap,
worn all day, all night,
he thinks only of his figure,
of slimming on sherbet and ginger ale—
more cut off from words than a seal.

This is the way day breaks in Bowditch Hall at McLean's;
the hooded night lights bring out "Bobbie,"
Porcellian '29,
a replica of Louis XVI
without the wig—
redolent and roly-poly as a sperm whale,
as he swashbuckles about in his birthday suit
and horses at chairs.
These victorious figures of bravado ossified young.

In between the limits of day,
hours and hours go by under the crew haircuts
and slightly too little nonsensical bachelor twinkle
of the Roman Catholic attendants.
(There are no Mayflower
screwballs in the Catholic Church.)

After a hearty New England breakfast,
I weigh two hundred pounds

this morning. Cock of the walk,
I strut in my turtle-necked French sailor's jersey
before the metal shaving mirrors,
and see the shaky future grow familiar
in the pinched, indigenous faces
of these thoroughbred mental cases,
twice my age and half my weight.
We are all old-timers,
each of us holds a locked razor.

MEMORIES OF WEST STREET AND LEPKE

Only teaching on Tuesdays, book-worming
in pajamas fresh from the washer each morning,
I hog a whole house on Boston's
"hardly passionate Marlborough Street,"
where even the man
scavenging filth in the back alley trash cans,
has two children, a beach wagon, a helpmate,
and is a "young Republican."
I have a nine months' daughter,
young enough to be my granddaughter.
Like the sun she rises in her flame-flamingo infants' wear.

These are the tranquillized *Fifties,*
and I am forty. Ought I to regret my seedtime?
I was a fire-breathing Catholic C. O.,
and made my manic statement,
telling off the state and president, and then
sat waiting sentence in the bull pen
beside a Negro boy with curlicues
of marijuana in his hair.

Given a year,
I walked on the roof of the West Street Jail, a short
enclosure like my school soccer court,

and saw the Hudson River once a day
through sooty clothesline entanglements
and bleaching khaki tenements.
Strolling, I yammered metaphysics with Abramowitz,
a jaundice-yellow ("it's really tan")
and fly-weight pacifist,
so vegetarian,
he wore rope shoes and preferred fallen fruit.
He tried to convert Bioff and Brown,
the Hollywood pimps, to his diet.
Hairy, muscular, suburban,
wearing chocolate double-breasted suits,
they blew their tops and beat him black and blue.

I was so out of things, I'd never heard
of the Jehovah's Witnesses.
"Are you a C. O.?" I asked a fellow jailbird.
"No," he answered, "I'm a J. W."
He taught me the "hospital tuck,"
and pointed out the T-shirted back
of *Murder Incorporated*'s Czar Lepke,
there piling towels on a rack,
or dawdling off to his little segregated cell full
of things forbidden the common man:
a portable radio, a dresser, two toy American
flags tied together with a ribbon of Easter palm.
Flabby, bald, lobotomized,
he drifted in a sheepish calm,
where no agonizing reappraisal
jarred his concentration on the electric chair—
hanging like an oasis in his air
of lost connections. . . .

MAN AND WIFE

Tamed by *Miltown,* we lie on Mother's bed;
the rising sun in war paint dyes us red;
in broad daylight her gilded bed-posts shine,
abandoned, almost Dionysian.
At last the trees are green on Marlborough Street,
blossoms on our magnolia ignite
the morning with their murderous five days' white.
All night I've held your hand,
as if you had
a fourth time faced the kingdom of the mad—
its hackneyed speech, its homicidal eye—
and dragged me home alive. . . . Oh my *Petite,*
clearest of all God's creatures, still all air and nerve:
you were in your twenties, and I,
once hand on glass
and heart in mouth,
outdrank the Rahvs in the heat
of Greenwich Village, fainting at your feet—
too boiled and shy
and poker-faced to make a pass,
while the shrill verve
of your invective scorched the traditional South.

Now twelve years later, you turn your back.
Sleepless, you hold
your pillow to your hollows like a child;
your old-fashioned tirade—
loving, rapid, merciless—
breaks like the Atlantic Ocean on my head.

SKUNK HOUR

Nautilus Island's hermit
heiress still lives through winter in her Spartan cottage;
her sheep still graze above the sea.
Her son's a bishop. Her farmer
is first selectman in our village;
she's in her dotage.

Thirsting for
the hierarchic privacy
of Queen Victoria's century,
she buys up all
the eyesores facing her shore,
and lets them fall.

The season's ill—
we've lost our summer millionaire,
who seemed to leap from an L. L. Bean
catalogue. His nine-knot yawl
was auctioned off to lobstermen.
A red fox stain covers Blue Hill.

And now our fairy
decorator brightens his shop for fall;
his fishnet's filled with orange cork,
orange, his cobbler's bench and awl;
there is no money in his work,
he'd rather marry.

One dark night,
my Tudor Ford climbed the hill's skull;
I watched for love-cars. Lights turned down,
they lay together, hull to hull,
where the graveyard shelves on the town. . . .
My mind's not right.

A car radio bleats,
"Love, O careless Love. . . ." I hear
my ill-spirit sob in each blood cell,
as if my hand were at its throat. . . .
I myself am hell;
nobody's here—

only skunks, that search
in the moonlight for a bite to eat.
They march on their soles up Main Street:
white stripes, moonstruck eyes' red fire
under the chalk-dry and spar spire
of the Trinitarian Church.

I stand on top
of our back steps and breathe the rich air—
a mother skunk with her column of kittens swills the garbage
    pail.
She jabs her wedge-head in a cup
of sour cream, drops her ostrich tail,
and will not scare.

WATER

It was a Maine lobster town—
each morning boatloads of hands
pushed off for granite
quarries on the islands,

and left dozens of bleak
white frame houses stuck
like oyster shells
on a hill of rock,

and below us, the sea lapped
the raw little match-stick

mazes of a weir,
where the fish for bait were trapped.

Remember? We sat on a slab of rock.
From this distance in time,
it seems the color
of iris, rotting and turning purpler,

but it was only
the usual gray rock
turning the usual green
when drenched by the sea.

The sea drenched the rock
at our feet all day,
and kept tearing away
flake after flake.

One night you dreamed
you were a mermaid clinging to a wharf-pile,
and trying to pull
off the barnacles with your hands.

We wished our two souls
might return like gulls
to the rock. In the end,
the water was too cold for us.

THE OLD FLAME

My old flame, my wife!
Remember our lists of birds?
One morning last summer, I drove
by our house in Maine. It was still
on top of its hill—

Now a red ear of Indian maize
was splashed on the door.
Old Glory with thirteen stars
hung on a pole. The clapboard
was old-red schoolhouse red.

Inside, a new landlord,
a new wife, a new broom!
Atlantic seaboard antique shop
pewter and plunder
shone in each room.

A new frontier!
No running next door
now to phone the sheriff
for his taxi to Bath
and the State Liquor Store!

No one saw your ghostly
imaginary lover
stare through the window,
and tighten
the scarf at his throat.

Health to the new people,
health to their flag, to their old
restored house on the hill!
Everything had been swept bare,
furnished, garnished, and aired.

Everything's changed for the best—
how quivering and fierce we were,
there snowbound together,
simmering like wasps
in our tent of books!

Poor ghost, old love, speak
with your old voice

of flaming insight
that kept us awake all night.
In one bed and apart,

we heard the plow
groaning up hill—
a red light, then a blue,
as it tossed off the snow
to the side of the road.

THE MOUTH OF THE HUDSON

[FOR ESTHER BROOKS]

A single man stands like a bird-watcher,
and scuffles the pepper and salt snow
from a discarded, gray
Westinghouse Electric cable drum.
He cannot discover America by counting
the chains of condemned freight-trains
from thirty states. They jolt and jar
and junk in the siding below him.
He has trouble with his balance.
His eyes drop,
and he drifts with the wild ice
ticking seaward down the Hudson,
like the blank sides of a jig-saw puzzle.

The ice ticks seaward like a clock.
A Negro toasts
wheat-seeds over the coke-fumes
of a punctured barrel.
Chemical air
sweeps in from New Jersey,
and smells of coffee.

Across the river,
ledges of suburban factories tan

in the sulphur-yellow sun
of the unforgivable landscape.

ALFRED CORNING CLARK

[1916–1961]

You read the *New York Times*
every day at recess,
but in its dry
obituary, a list
of your wives, nothing is news,
except the ninety-five
thousand dollar engagement ring
you gave the sixth.
Poor rich boy,
you were unreasonably adult
at taking your time,
and died at forty-five.
Poor Al Clark,
behind your enlarged,
hardly recognizable photograph,
I feel the pain.
You were alive. You are dead.
You wore bow-ties and dark
blue coats, and sucked
wintergreen or cinnamon lifesavers
to sweeten your breath.
There must be something—
some one to praise
your triumphant diffidence,
your refusal of exertion,
the intelligence
that pulsed in the sensitive,
pale concavities of your forehead.
You never worked,
and were third in the form.

I owe you something—
I was befogged,
and you were too bored,
quick and cool to laugh.
You are dear to me, Alfred;
our reluctant souls united
in our unconventional
illegal games of chess
on the St. Mark's quadrangle.
You usually won—
motionless
as a lizard in the sun.

THE DRINKER

The man is killing time—there's nothing else.
No help now from the fifth of Bourbon
chucked helter-skelter into the river,
even its cork sucked under.

Stubbed before-breakfast cigarettes
burn bull's-eyes on the bedside table;
a plastic tumbler of alka seltzer
champagnes in the bathroom.

No help from his body, the whale's
warm-hearted blubber, foundering down
leagues of ocean, gasping whiteness.
The barbed hooks fester. The lines snap tight.

When he looks for neighbors, their names blur in the
    window,
his distracted eye sees only glass sky.
His despair has the galvanized color
of the mop and water in the galvanized bucket.

Once she was close to him
as water to the dead metal.

He looks at her engagements inked on her calendar.
A list of indictments.
At the numbers in her thumbed black telephone book.
A quiver full of arrows.

Her absence hisses like steam,
the pipes sing . . .
even corroded metal somehow functions.
He snores in his iron lung,

and hears the voice of Eve,
beseeching freedom from the Garden's
perfect and ponderous bubble. No voice
outsings the serpent's flawed, euphoric hiss.

The cheese wilts in the rat-trap,
the milk turns to junket in the cornflakes bowl,
car keys and razor blades
shine in an ashtray.

Is he killing time? Out on the street,
two cops on horseback clop through the April rain
to check the parking meter violations—
their oilskins yellow as forsythia.

SOFT WOOD

[FOR HARRIET WINSLOW]

Sometimes I have supposed seals
must live as long as the Scholar Gypsy.
Even in their barred pond at the zoo they are happy,
and no sunflower turns
more delicately to the sun
without a wincing of the will.

Here too in Maine things bend to the wind forever.
After two years away, one must get used
to the painted soft wood staying bright and clean,
to the air blasting an all-white wall whiter,
as it blows through curtain and screen
touched with salt and evergreen.

The green juniper berry spills crystal-clear gin,
and even the hot water in the bathtub
is more than water,
and rich with the scouring effervescence
of something healing,
the illimitable salt.

Things last, but sometimes for days here
only children seem fit to handle children,
and there is no utility or inspiration
in the wind smashing without direction.
The fresh paint
on the captains' houses hides softer wood.

Their square-riggers used to whiten
the four corners of the globe,
but it's no consolation to know
the possessors seldom outlast the possessions,
once warped and mothered by their touch.
Shed skin will never fit another wearer.

Yet the seal pack will bark past my window
summer after summer.
This is the season
when our friends may and will die daily.
Surely the lives of the old
are briefer than the young.

Harriet Winslow, who owned this house,
was more to me than my mother.

I think of you far off in Washington,
breathing in the heat wave
and air-conditioning, knowing
each drug that numbs alerts another nerve to pain.

FOR THE UNION DEAD

"RELINQUUNT OMNIA SERVARE REM PUBLICAM."

The old South Boston Aquarium stands
in a Sahara of snow now. Its broken windows are boarded.
The bronze weathervane cod has lost half its scales.
The airy tanks are dry.

Once my nose crawled like a snail on the glass;
my hand tingled
to burst the bubbles
drifting from the noses of the cowed, compliant fish.

My hand draws back. I often sigh still
for the dark downward and vegetating kingdom
of the fish and reptile. One morning last March,
I pressed against the new barbed and galvanized

fence on the Boston Common. Behind their cage,
yellow dinosaur steamshovels were grunting
as they cropped up tons of mush and grass
to gouge their underworld garage.

Parking spaces luxuriate like civic
sandpiles in the heart of Boston.
A girdle of orange, Puritan-pumpkin colored girders
braces the tingling Statehouse,

shaking over the excavations, as it faces Colonel Shaw
and his bell-cheeked Negro infantry
on St. Gaudens' shaking Civil War relief,
propped by a plank splint against the garage's earthquake.

Two months after marching through Boston,
half the regiment was dead;
at the dedication,
William James could almost hear the bronze Negroes breathe.

Their monument sticks like a fishbone
in the city's throat.
Its Colonel is as lean
as a compass-needle.

He has an angry wrenlike vigilance,
a greyhound's gentle tautness;
he seems to wince at pleasure,
and suffocate for privacy.

He is out of bounds now. He rejoices in man's lovely,
peculiar power to choose life and die—
when he leads his black soldiers to death,
he cannot bend his back.

On a thousand small town New England greens,
the old white churches hold their air
of sparse, sincere rebellion; frayed flags
quilt the graveyards of the Grand Army of the Republic.

The stone statues of the abstract Union Soldier
grow slimmer and younger each year—
wasp-waisted, they doze over muskets
and muse through their sideburns . . .

Shaw's father wanted no monument
except the ditch,
where his son's body was thrown
and lost with his "niggers."

The ditch is nearer.
There are no statues for the last war here;

on Boylston Street, a commercial photograph
shows Hiroshima boiling

over a Mosler Safe, the "Rock of Ages"
that survived the blast. Space is nearer.
When I crouch to my television set,
the drained faces of Negro school-children rise like balloons.

Colonel Shaw
is riding on his bubble,
he waits
for the blessèd break.

The Aquarium is gone. Everywhere,
giant finned cars nose forward like fish;
a savage servility
slides by on grease.

MARGARET FULLER DROWNED

You had everything to rattle the men who wrote.
The first American woman? Margaret Fuller . . .
in a white nightgown, your hair fallen long
at the foot of the foremast, you just forty,
your husband Angelo thirty, your Angelino one—
all drowned with brief anguish together. . . . Your fire-call,
your voice, was like thorns crackling under a pot,
you knew the Church burdens and infects as all dead forms,
however gallant and lovely in their life;
progress is not by renunciation.
"Myself," you wrote, "is all I know of heaven.
With my intellect, I always can
and always shall make out, but that's not half—
the life, the life, O my God, will life never be sweet?"

WILLIAM CARLOS WILLIAMS

Who loved more? William Carlos Williams,
in collegiate black slacks, gabardine coat,
and loafers polished like rosewood on yachts,
straying stonefoot through his town-end garden,
man and flower seedy with three autumn strokes,
his brown, horned eyes enlarged, an ant's, through glasses;
his Mother, stonedeaf, her face a wizened talon,
her hair the burnt-out ash of lush Puerto Rican grass;
her black, blind, bituminous eye inquisitorial.
"Mama," he says, "which would you rather see here,
me or two blondes?" Then later, "The old bitch
is over a hundred, I'll kick off tomorrow."
He said, "I am sixty-seven, and more
attractive to girls than when I was seventeen."

ROBERT FROST

Robert Frost at midnight, the audience gone
to vapor, the great act laid on the shelf in mothballs,
his voice is musical and raw—he writes in the flyleaf:
For Robert from Robert, his friend in the art.
"Sometimes I feel too full of myself," I say.
And he, misunderstanding, "When I am low,
I stray away. My son wasn't your kind. The night
we told him Merrill Moore would come to treat him,
he said, 'I'll kill him first.' One of my daughters thought
    things,
thought every male she met was out to make her;
the way she dressed, she couldn't make a whorehouse."
And I, "Sometimes I'm so happy I can't ·stand myself."
And he, "When I am too full of joy, I think
how little good my health did anyone near me."

Will Not Come Back

[AFTER BECQUER]

Dark swallows will doubtless come back killing
the injudicious nightflies with a clack of the beak;
but these that stopped full flight to see your beauty
and my good fortune . . . as if they knew our names—
they'll not come back. The thick lemony honeysuckle,
climbing from the earthroot to your window,
will open more beautiful blossoms to the evening;
but these . . . like dewdrops, trembling, shining, falling,
the tears of day—they'll not come back. . . .
Some other love will sound his fireword for you
and wake your heart, perhaps, from its cool sleep;
but silent, absorbed, and on his knees,
as men adore God at the altar, as I love you—
don't blind yourself, you'll not be loved like that.

Elizabeth

An unaccustomed ripeness in the wood;
move but an inch and moldy splinters fall
in sawdust from the wall's aluminum paint,
once loud and fresh, now aged to weathered wood.
Squalls of the seagull's exaggerated outcry
dim out in the fog. . . . *Pace, pace.* All day our words
were rusty fish-hooks—wormwood . . . Dear Heart's-Ease,
we rest from all discussion, drinking, smoking,
pills for high blood, three pairs of glasses—soaking
in the sweat of our hard-earned supremacy,
offering a child our leathery love. We're fifty,
and free! Young, tottering on the dizzying brink
of discretion once, you wanted nothing,
but to be old, do nothing, type and think.

WORDS FOR MUFFIN, A GUINEA-PIG

"Of late they leave the light on in my entry,
so I won't scare, though I never scare in the dark;
I bless this arrow that flies from wall to window . . .
five years and a nightlight given me to breathe—
Heidegger said spare time is ecstasy. . . .
I am not scared, although my life was short;
my sickly breathing sounded like dry leather.
Mrs. Muffin! It clicks. I had my day.
You'll paint me like Cromwell with all my warts:
small mop with a tumor and eyes too popped for thought.
I was a rhinoceros when jumped by my sons.
I ate and bred, and then I only ate,
my life zenithed in the Lyndon Johnson 'sixties . . .
this short pound God threw on the scales, found wanting."

BRINGING A TURTLE HOME

On the road to Bangor, we spotted a domed stone,
a painted turtle petrified by fear.
I picked it up. The turtle had come a long walk,
200 millennia understudy to dinosaurs,
then their survivors. A god for the out-of-power. . . .
Faster gods come to Castine, flush yachtsmen who see
hell as a city very much like New York,
these gods give a bad past and worse future to men
who never bother to set a spinnaker;
culture without cash isn't worth their spit.
The laughter on Mount Olympus was always breezy. . . .
Goodnight, little Boy, little Soldier, live,
a toy to your friend, a stone of stumbling to God—
sandpaper Turtle, scratching your pail for water.

RETURNING TURTLE

Weeks hitting the road, one fasting in the bathtub,
raw hamburger mossing in the watery stoppage,
the room drenched with musk like kerosene—
no one shaved, and only the turtle washed.
He was so beautiful when we flipped him over:
greens, reds, yellows, fringe of the faded savage,
the last Sioux, old and worn, saying with weariness,
"Why doesn't the Great White Father put his red
children on wheels, and move us as he will?"
We drove to the Orland River, and watched the turtle
rush for water like rushing into marriage,
swimming in uncontaminated joy,
lovely the flies that fed that sleazy surface,
a turtle looking back at us, and blinking.

DOLPHIN

My Dolphin, you only guide me by surprise,
captive as Racine, the man of craft,
drawn through his maze of iron composition
by the incomparable wandering voice of Phèdre.
When I was troubled in mind, you made for my body
caught in its hangman's-knot of sinking lines,
the glassy bowing and scraping of my will. . . .
I have sat and listened to too many
words of the collaborating muse,
and plotted perhaps too freely with my life,
not avoiding injury to others,
not avoiding injury to myself—
to ask compassion . . . this book, half fiction,
an eelnet made by man for the eel fighting—

my eyes have seen what my hand did.

JOHN BERRYMAN

INTERVIEWER: You, along with Lowell, Sylvia Plath, and several others have been called a confessional poet. How do you react to that label?
BERRYMAN: With rage and contempt! Next question.

He could never be charged with the sort of foolish consistency that is said to be a sign of little minds. It is difficult, in fact, to conceive of a life more filled with inconsistencies than that of John Berryman. His productivity, to suggest an obvious contradiction, would clearly seem to be at odds with his thirty-year dependence on alcohol. An articulate man of enormous charm and personal magnetism, he was given to offending individuals (and audiences) from one coast to the other. A believer in monogamy, he married three times and, by his own admission, engaged in numerous adulterous liaisons. And this complex man, who spent his life lamenting the suicide that left him fatherless as a child, took his own life, leaving behind a young wife and two daughters, aged eight and one.

John Smith, the poet's singularly prosaic name during his early years, was born October 25, 1916, in a small Oklahoma town, the son of John Allyn Smith, a bank examiner, and his wife, Martha, a teacher. Since he worked the scorpion into his poems, one is struck, conditioned cynicism about matters astrological notwithstanding, by the persuasive place in the poet's life of the conventional Scorpio characteristics: dominating personality; powerful, difficult individuality; secretiveness; ruthlessness; inconsistency; charisma. Born three days earlier, he would have been an evenhanded Libra, and we would be without the more daring and passionate of his poems. Or so would say those who put their faith in celestial bodies. Picasso was also born on October 25.

While the family was living in Florida, the boy's father, depressed by business failures and marital problems, killed himself—his son apparently heard the shot. His widow later married another banker, named Berryman, and the boy became John Allyn McAlpin Berryman. After four unhappy years at South Kent, an Episcopal prep school in Connecticut, he attended Columbia, where he became a disciple of the poet Mark Van Doren and worked on the literary review with classmate Robert Giroux, later his editor at Farrar, Straus and Giroux. Following graduation, he studied for two years in England, where he met Yeats and Auden as well as Dylan Thomas, who became a pub-crawling companion.

On his return to the States, he held editing and teaching jobs (Wayne State University, Harvard, Princeton) and slowly acquired visibility as a critic and poet. New Directions published 2,000 copies of *Poems* in his twenty-eighth year, and though one prominent reviewer, Northrop Frye, dismissed the lyrics as "constipated elegance," the young poet was clearly on his way. His first marriage, to Eileen Simpson, is described in her novel *The Maze,* a roman à clef about a high-strung poet. While he and Simpson were still together he fell in love with a young married woman; it was during the period of their affair that his addiction to alcohol began. He kept a journal of the relationship, a sequence of 115 intimate sonnets. After years of indecision about whether to destroy these incriminating confessions of a "knock-down–drag-out love," he achieved enough emotional distance from the events they document to face the issue objectively:

> He made, a thousand years ago, a-many songs
> for an Excellent lady, wif whom he was in wuv,
> shall now he publish them?
> Has he the right, upon that old young man,
> to bare his nervous system
> & display all the clouds again as they were above?

He decides, finally, to "free them to the winds that play, / let boys & girls with these old songs have holiday / if they feel like it." The speaker in this sequence, comical, wildly inventive, and self-deprecating, suggests an early model for Henry, Berryman's great character in the *Dream Songs*.

His first major collection, *The Dispossessed*, consists of some stunning lyrics as well as several conventional, world-weary poems that seem to have been composed by a computer with weltschmerz. This collection, heavily influenced by Auden and Yeats, appeared in 1948, followed two years later by *Stephen Crane*, a psychoanalytic biography important in part for what it reveals about the poet himself. During 1952–53 he used the first of two Guggenheim Fellowships to work on *Homage to Mistress Bradstreet*, described in reviews as a "path-breaking master-piece," as "the poem of his generation" and, by Edmund Wilson, as "the most important long poem by an American since *The Waste Land*." Each of the poem's stanzas is composed of eight highly compressed lines, their measured, incantatory language suited to the drama they record, a dialogue taking place out of time and out of space between two poets, one living, the other, summoned from the seventeenth century, shimmering for an intense duet, and then disappearing. In these stanzas, typical of the work's fractured and imaginative language, the poet summons Anne's ghost:

> Outside the New World winters in grand dark
> white air lashing high thro' the virgin stands
> foxes down foxholes sigh,
> surely the English heart quails, stunned.
> I doubt if Simon than this blast, that sea,
> spares from his rigour for your poetry
> more. We are on each other's hands
> who care. Both of our worlds unhanded us. Lie stark,
>
> thy eyes look to me mild. Out of maize & air
> your body's made, and moves. I summon, see,
> from the centuries it.
> I think you won't stay. How do we
> linger, diminished, on our lovers' air,

implausibly visible, to whom, a year,
years, over interims; or not;
to a long stranger; or not; shimmer & disappear.

Berryman's relationship with "Lise," his mistress in the *Sonnets,*
an adulterous love that dared not speak its name, is celebrated in
language that is often glib, colloquial, racy. Anne Bradstreet, on
the other hand, more muse than mistress, is the object of intensi-
ties more aesthetic than physical. The poem, to be sure, is
couched as an adulterous seduction—the poet wooing Anne not
only out of history but away from her husband and family—but
the relationship, charming and literary, raises no questions about
moral behavior. While the *Sonnets* celebrate a physical relation-
ship, *Homage to Mistress Bradstreet* is a celebration of art, of the
power of the imagination to transcend the limitations of the
flesh. Here, in Berryman's fresh and idiosyncratic idiom, is
Anne's voice shortly before she disappears:

My window gives on the graves, in our great new house
(how many burned?) upstairs, among the elms.
I lie, & endure, & wonder.
A haze slips sometimes over my dreams
and holiness on horses' bells shall stand.
Wandering pacemaker, unsteadying friend,
in a redskin calm I wait:
beat when you will our end. Sinkings & droopings drowse.

The work was published in 1956, the same year Berryman
was divorced from Eileen Simpson and married Ann Levine, the
mother of his son, Paul, born in 1957. This marriage lasted four
years. From 1956 until his death seventeen years later he taught
at the University of Minnesota, giving courses on a wide range
of subjects, including the history of ideas, American civilization,
Shakespeare, and Dante. His eloquence, learning, and passion
earned him a reputation as an inspiring teacher; Philip Levine,
his student at the University of Iowa, describes him as "the most
brilliant, intense, articulate man I've ever met."

In 1960, Berryman, then forty-six, was divorced again, and the following year he married Kathleen Donohue. Four years later 77 *Dream Songs,* long in the making, appeared to critical acclaim and went on to win a Pulitzer prize. These haunting first-person lyrics, each in eighteen lines—a kind of expanded sonnet—document the chaotic and hilarious life-in-progress of Henry (also called Pussycat and Mr. Bones), a vulnerable, eccentric character whose days, much like those of his creator, are filled with self-pity, rage, laughter, resentment, and love, all expressed in a brilliantly quirky language that combines vulgar colloquialisms with high Shakespearean rhetoric. The songs emerged almost spontaneously over a period of many years: sitting up night after night, puffing on Tareytons and drinking either bourbon or coffee, the poet, speaking through what Lowell called his "ventriloquist's doll," brought forth hundreds of them, in the process scattering pages (and ashes) all over the rug.

Berryman spent 1966 in Dublin, supported by a second Guggenheim Fellowship and an award from the National Endowment for the Arts. Two years later *His Toy, His Dream, His Rest,* consisting of 308 more dream songs, was published. Robert Lowell commented that while 77 *Dream Songs* "are harder than most hard modern poetry," the succeeding poems in *His Toy* "are as direct as a prose journal, as readable as poetry can be." The book received an enormous amount of attention and won the National Book Award in 1969, the same year Berryman was selected to share the Bollingen Award with Karl Shapiro. His publisher immediately published all 385 songs in a single volume. The collected *Dream Songs,* for all their self-indulgence and high jinks, evoke the sort of pity and fear that can be cathartic for the reader willing to listen attentively to Henry's idiosyncratic music. A point I stressed in my own 1977 book about the poet still seems valid to me:

> Our lives are all potentially disastrous, and artists like Berryman and Lowell who live perilously close to the abyss make it possible for us to journey over threatening terrain, to experience its terror, and to return intact. Literature does not tell us anything;

it permits us to participate in a life, to share an angle of vision, and often to make some crucial personal discoveries. In courting certain kinds of disaster, Henry spares us the necessity of doing so for ourselves, overpowering as the attractions sometimes are.

Love & Fame followed in 1970. In this sequence of often shocking confessional poems Berryman dispenses with his alter ego, Henry, and speaks directly about himself.

> Reflexions on suicide, & on my father, possess me.
> I drink too much. My wife threatens separation.
> She won't 'nurse' me. She feels 'inadequate'.
> We don't mix together.

A number of previously sympathetic critics responded to the work with scorn, bitter medicine to a thin-skinned man who thirsted for approbation. During the next year, while working on a biography of Shakespeare, he was in and out of a Minneapolis hospital (which he referred to as Werewolf Hills), remaining for weeks at a time as part of a therapy group that adopted the twelve steps formulated by Alcoholics Anonymous. During this period Berryman wrote the poems, mostly religious, published posthumously in *Delusions, Etc.*

> I don't think I will sing
>
> any more just now;
> or ever. I must start
> to sit with a blind brow
> above an empty heart.

He also began a thinly veiled autobiographical novel, *Recovery,* also published after his death.

The poet ended his life on January 7, 1972, by jumping from a bridge onto some frozen rocks on the bank of the Mississippi River. He was fifty-seven. Throughout his life he was, by all reports, a dynamo of unstoppable energy (Mark Van Doren said that as a student Berryman "sometimes seemed to be composed of nothing but bristles and points"), but, his father's fatal heir, he finally lost the will to inhabit the body he had abused for so long.

Collected Poems, 1937–1971, edited by Charles Thornbury (Farrar, Straus and Giroux, 1989); *The Dream Songs* (Farrar, Straus and Giroux, 1969); *Homage to Mistress Bradstreet and Other Poems* (Farrar, Straus and Giroux, 1968); *Berryman's Sonnets* (Farrar, Straus and Giroux, 1967); *Recovery* (novel; Farrar, Straus and Giroux, 1973). Paul Mariani, *Dream Song: The Life of John Berryman* (William Morrow & Co., 1990); Eileen Simpson, *The Maze* (Simon and Schuster, 1975). For criticism, see Joel Conarroe, *John Berryman: An Introduction to the Poetry* (Columbia University Press, 1977); *Berryman's Understanding: Reflections on the Poetry of John Berryman,* edited by Harry Thomas (Northeastern University Press, 1988).

THE TRAVELLER

They pointed me out on the highway, and they said
'That man has a curious way of holding his head.'

They pointed me out on the beach; they said 'That man
Will never become as we are, try as he can.'

They pointed me out at the station, and the guard
Looked at me twice, thrice, thoughtfully & hard.

I took the same train that the others took,
To the same place. Were it not for that look
And those words, we were all of us the same.
I studied merely maps. I tried to name
The effects of motion on the travellers,
I watched the couple I could see, the curse
And blessings of that couple, their destination,

The deception practised on them at the station,
Their courage. When the train stopped and they knew
The end of their journey, I descended too.

THE ANIMAL TRAINER (1)

I told him: The time has come, I must be gone.
It is time to leave the circus and circus days,
The admissions, the menagerie, the drums,
Excitements of disappointment and praise.
In a suburb of the spirit I shall seize
The steady and exalted light of the sun,
And live there, out of the tension that decays,
Until I become a man alone of noon.

Heart said: Can you do without your animals?
The looking, licking, smelling animals?
The friendly fumbling beast? The listening one?
That standing up and worst of animals?
What will become of you in the pure light
When all your enemies are gone, and gone
The inexhaustible prospect of the night?

—But the night is now the body of my fear,
These animals are my distraction. Once
Let me escape the smells and cages here,
Once let me stand naked in the sun,
All these performances will be forgotten.
I shall concentrate in the sunlight there.

Said the conservative Heart: Your animals
Are occupation, food for you, your love
And your immense responsibility;
They are the travellers by which you live.
(Without you they will pace and pine, or die.)

—I reared them, tended them (I said) and still
They plague me, they will not perform, they run
Into forbidden corners, they fight, they steal.
Better to live like an artist in the sun.

—You are an animal trainer, Heart replied.
Without your animals leaping at your side
No sun will save you, nor this bloodless pride.

—What must I do then? Must I stay and work
With animals, and confront the night, in the circus?

—You léarn from animals. You léarn in the dark.

A PROFESSOR'S SONG

(. . rabid or dog-dull.) Let me tell you how
The Eighteenth Century couplet ended. Now
Tell me. Troll me the sources of that Song—
Assigned last week—by Blake. Come, come along,
Gentlemen. (Fidget and huddle, do. Squint soon.)
I want to end these fellows all by noon.

'That deep romantic chasm'—an early use;
The word is from the French, by our abuse
Fished out a bit. (Red all your eyes. O when?)
'A poet is a man speaking to men':
But I am then a poet, am I not?—
Ha ha. The radiator, please. Well, what?

Alive now—no—Blake would have written prose,
But movement following movement crisply flows,
So much the better, better the much so,
As burbleth Mozart. Twelve. The class can go.
Until I meet you, then, in Upper Hell
Convulsed, foaming immortal blood: farewell.

He made, a thousand years ago, a-many songs
for an Excellent lady, wif whom he was in wuv,
shall now he publish them?
Has he the right, upon that old young man,
to bare his nervous system
& display all the clouds again as they were above?

As a friend of the Court I would say, Let them die.
What does anything matter? Burn them up,
put them in a bank vault.
I thought of that and when I returned to this country
I took them out again. The original fault
will not be undone by fire.

The original fault was whether wickedness
was soluble in art. History says it is,
Jacques Maritain says it is,
barely. So free them to the winds that play,
let boys & girls with these old songs have holiday
if they feel like it.

Sonnet 13

I lift—lift you five States away your glass,
Wide of this bar you never graced, where none
Ever I know came, where what work is done
Even by these men I know not, where a brass
Police-car sign peers in, wet strange cars pass,
Soiled hangs the rag of day out over this town,
A juke-box brains air where I drink alone,
The spruce barkeep sports a toupee alas—

My glass I lift at six o'clock, my darling,
As you plotted . . Chinese couples shift in bed,

We shared today not even filthy weather,
Beasts in the hills their tigerish love are snarling,
Suddenly they clash, I blow my short ash red,
Grey eyes light! and we have our drink together.

Sonnet 23

They may, because I would not cloy your ear—
If ever these songs by other ears are heard—
With 'love'; suppose I loved you not, but blurred
Lust with strange images, warm, not quite sincere,
To switch a bedroom black. O mutineer
With me against these empty captains! gird
Your scorn again above all at *this* word
Pompous and vague on the stump of his career.

Also I fox 'heart', striking a modern breast
Hollow as a drum, and 'beauty' I taboo;
I want a verse fresh as a bubble breaks,
As little false . . Blood of my sweet unrest
Runs all the same—I am in love with you—
Trapped in my rib-cage something throes and aches!

Sonnet 115

As usual I'm up before the sun
begins to warm this intolerable place
and I have stared all night upon your face
but am not wiser thereby. Everyone
rattles his weakness or his thing undone,
I shake you like a rat. Open disgrace
yawns all before me: have I left a trace,
a spoor? Clouding it over, I look for my gun.

She's hidden it. I won't sing on of that.
Whiskey is bracing. Failures are my speed,

I thrive on ends, the dog is at the door
in heat, the neighbourhood is male except one cat
and they thresh on my stoop. Prevent my need,
Someone, and come & find me on the floor.

Homage to Mistress Bradstreet

[1953]

*[Born 1612 Anne Dudley, married at 16
Simon Bradstreet, a Cambridge man,
steward to the Countess of Warwick &
protégé of her father Thomas Dudley
secretary to the Earl of Lincoln.
Crossed in the Arbella, 1630, under
Governor Winthrop.]*

[1]

The Governor your husband lived so long
moved you not, restless, waiting for him? Still,
you were a patient woman.—
I seem to see you pause here still:
Sylvester, Quarles, in moments odd you pored
before a fire at, bright eyes on the Lord,
all the children still.
'Simon . . .' Simon will listen while you read a Song.

[2]

Outside the New World winters in grand dark
white air lashing high thro' the virgin stands
foxes down foxholes sigh,
surely the English heart quails, stunned.
I doubt if Simon than this blast, that sea,
spares from his rigour for your poetry
more. We are on each other's hands
who care. Both of our worlds unhanded us. Lie stark,

[3]

thy eyes look to me mild. Out of maize & air
your body's made, and moves. I summon, see,
from the centuries it.
I think you won't stay. How do we
linger, diminished, in our lovers' air,
implausibly visible, to whom, a year,
years, over interims; or not;
to a long stranger; or not; shimmer & disappear.

[4]

Jaw-ript, rot with its wisdom, rending then;
then not. When the mouth dies, who misses you?
Your master never died,
Simon ah thirty years past you—
Pockmarkt & westward staring on a haggard deck
it seems I find you, young. I come to check,
I come to stay with you,
and the Governor, & Father, & Simon, & the huddled men.

[5]

By the week we landed we were, most, used up.
Strange ships across us, after a fortnight's winds
unfavouring, frightened us;
bone-sad cold, sleet, scurvy; so were ill
many as one day we could have no sermons;
broils, quelled; a fatherless child unkennelled; vermin
crowding & waiting: waiting.
And the day itself he leapt ashore young Henry Winthrop

[6]

(delivered from the waves; because he found
off their wigwams, sharp-eyed, a lone canoe
across a tidal river,
that water glittered fair & blue
& narrow, none of the other men could swim
and the plantation's prime theft up to him,

shouldered on a glad day
hard on the glorious feasting of thanksgiving) drowned.

[7]

How long with nothing in the ruinous heat,
clams & acorns stomaching, distinction perishing,
at which my heart rose,
with brackish water, we would sing.
When whispers knew the Governor's last bread
was browning in his oven, we were discourag'd.
The Lady Arbella dying—
dyings—at which my heart   rose, but I did submit.

[8]

That beyond the Atlantic wound our woes enlarge
is hard, hard that starvation burnishes our fear,
but I do gloss for You.
Strangers & pilgrims fare we here,
declaring we seek a City. Shall we be deceived?
I know whom I have trusted, & whom I have believed,
and that he is able to
keep   that I have committed to his charge.

[9]

Winter than summer worse, that first, like a file
on a quick, or the poison suck of a thrilled tooth;
and still we may unpack.
Wolves & storms among, uncouth
board-pieces, boxes, barrels vanish, grow
houses, rise. Motes that hop in sunlight slow
indoors, and I am Ruth
away: open my mouth, my eyes wet: I would smile:

[10]

vellum I palm, and dream. Their forest dies
to greensward, privets, elms & towers, whence
a nightingale is throbbing.

Women sleep sound. I was happy once . .
(Something keeps on not happening; I shrink?)
These minutes all their passions & powers sink
and I am not one chance
for an unknown cry or a flicker of unknown eyes.

[11]

Chapped souls ours, by the day Spring's strong winds swelled,
Jack's pulpits arched, more glad. The shawl I pinned
flaps like a shooting soul
might in such weather Heaven send.
Succumbing half, in spirit, to a salmon sash
I prod the nerveless novel succotash—
I must be disciplined,
in arms, against that one, and our dissidents, and myself.

[12]

Versing, I shroud among the dynasties;
quaternion on quaternion, tireless I phrase
anything past, dead, far,
sacred, for a barbarous place.
—To please your wintry father? all this bald
abstract didactic rime I read appalled
harassed for your fame
mistress neither of fiery nor velvet verse, on your knees

[13]

hopeful & shamefast, chaste, laborious, odd,
whom the sea tore.—The damned roar with loss,
so they hug & are mean
with themselves, and I cannot be thus.
Why then do I repine, sick, bad, to long
after what must not be? I lie wrong
once more. For at fourteen
I found my heart more carnal and sitting loose from God,

[14]

vanity & the follies of youth took hold of me;
then the pox blasted, when the Lord returned.
That year for my sorry face
so-much-older Simon burned,
so Father smiled, with love. Their will be done.
He to me ill lingeringly, learning to shun
a bliss, a lightning blood
vouchsafed, what did seem life. I kissed his Mystery.

[15]

Drydust in God's eye the aquavivid skin
of Simon snoring lit with fountaining dawn
when my eyes unlid, sad.
John Cotton shines on Boston's sin—
I ám drawn, in pieties that seem
the weary drizzle of an unremembered dream.
Women have gone mad
at twenty-one. Ambition mines, atrocious, in.

[16]

Food endless, people few, all to be done.
As pippins roast, the question of the wolves
turns & turns.
Fangs of a wolf will keep, the neck
round of a child, that child brave. I remember who
in meeting smiled & was punisht, and I know who
whispered & was stockt.
We lead a thoughtful life. But Boston's cage we shun.

[17]

The winters close, Springs open, no child stirs
under my withering heart, O seasoned heart
God grudged his aid.
All things else soil like a shirt.
Simon is much away. My executive stales.
The town came through for the cartway by the pales,

but my patience is short.
I revolt from, I am like, these savage foresters

[18]

whose passionless dicker in the shade, whose glance
impassive & scant, belie their murderous cries
when quarry seems to show.
Again I must have been wrong, twice.
Unwell in a new way. Can that begin?
God brandishes. O love, O I love. Kin,
gather. My world is strange
and merciful, ingrown months, blessing a swelling trance.

[19]

So squeezed, wince you I scream? I love you & hate
off with you. Ages! *Useless.* Below my waist
he has me in Hell's vise.
Stalling. He let go. Come back: brace
me somewhere. No. No. Yes! everything down
hardens I press with horrible joy down
my back cracks like a wrist
shame I am voiding oh behind it is too late

[20]

hide me forever I work thrust I must free
now I all muscles & bones concentrate
what is living from dying?
Simon I must leave you so untidy
Monster you are killing me Be sure
I'll have you later Women do endure
I can *can* no longer
and it passes the wretched trap whelming and I am me

[21]

drencht & powerful, I did it with my body!
One proud tug greens Heaven. Marvellous,
unforbidding Majesty.

Swell, imperious bells. I fly.
Mountainous, woman not breaks and will bend:
sways God nearby: anguish comes to an end.
Blossomed Sarah, and I
blossom. Is that thing alive? I hear a famisht howl.

[22]

Beloved household, I am Simon's wife,
and the mother of Samuel—whom greedy yet I miss
out of his kicking place.
More in some ways I feel at a loss,
freer. Cantabanks & mummers, nears
longing for you. Our chopping scores my ears,
our costume bores my eyes.
St. George to the good sword, rise! chop-logic's rife

[23]

& fever & Satan & Satan's ancient fere.
Pioneering is not feeling well,
not Indians, beasts.
Not all their riddling can forestall
one leaving. Sam, your uncle has had to
go fróm us to live with God. 'Then Aunt went too?'
Dear, she does wait still.
Stricken: 'Oh. Then he takes   us one by one.' My dear.

[24]

Forswearing it otherwise, they starch their minds.
Folkmoots, & blether, blether. John Cotton rakes
to the synod of Cambridge.
Down from my body my legs flow,
out from it arms wave, on it my head shakes.
Now Mistress Hutchinson rings forth a call—
should she? many creep out at a broken wall—
affirming the Holy Ghost
dwells in one justified. Factioning passion blinds

[25]

all to all her good, all—can she be exiled?
Bitter sister, victim! I miss you.
—I miss you, Anne,
day or night weak as a child,
tender & empty, doomed, quick to no tryst.
—I hear you. Be kind, you who leaguer
my image in the mist.
—Be kind you, to one unchained eager far & wild

[26]

and if, O my love, my heart is breaking, please
neglect my cries and I will spare you. Deep
in Time's grave, Love's, you lie still.
Lie still. —Now? That happy shape
my forehead had under my most long, rare,
ravendark, hidden, soft bodiless hair
you award me still.
You must not love me, but   I do not bid you cease.

[27]

Veiled my eyes, attending. How can it be I?
Moist, with parted lips, I listen, wicked.
I shake in the morning & retch.
Brood I do on myself naked.
A fading world I dust, with fingers new.
—I have earned the right to be alone with you.
—What right can that be?
Convulsing, if you love, enough, like a sweet lie.

[28]

Not that, I know, you can. This cratered skin,
like the crabs & shells of my Palissy ewer, touch!
Oh, you do, you do?
Falls on me what I like a witch,
for lawless holds, annihilations of law
which Time and he and man abhor, foresaw:

sharper than what my Friend
brought me for my revolt when I moved smooth & thin,

[29]

faintings black, rigour, chilling, brown
parching, back, brain burning, the grey pocks
itch, a manic stench
of pustules snapping, pain floods the palm,
sleepless, or a red shaft with a dreadful start
rides at the chapel, like a slipping heart.
My soul strains in one qualm
ah but *this* is not to save me but to throw me down.

[30]

And out of this I lull. It lessens. Kiss me.
That once. As sings out up in sparkling dark
a trail of a star & dies,
while the breath flutters, sounding, mark,
so shorn ought such caresses to us be
who, deserving nothing, flush and flee
the darkness of that light,
a lurching frozen from a warm dream. Talk to me.

[31]

—It is Spring's New England. Pussy willows wedge
up in the wet. Milky crestings, fringed
yellow, in heaven, eyed
by the melting hand-in-hand or mere
desirers single, heavy-footed, rapt,
make surge poor human hearts. Venus is trapt—
the hefty pike shifts, sheer—
in Orion blazing. Warblings, odours, nudge to an edge—

[32]

—Ravishing, ha, what crouches outside ought,
flamboyant, ill, angelic. Often, now,
I am afraid of you.

I am a sobersides; I know.
I *want* to take you for my lover. —Do.
—I hear a madness. Harmless I to you
am not, not I? —No.
—I cannot but be. Sing a concord of our thought.

[33]
—Wan dolls in indigo on gold: refrain
my western lust. I am drowning in this past.
I lose sight of you
who mistress me from air. Unbraced
in delirium of the grand depths, giving away
haunters what kept me, I breathe solid spray.
—I am losing you!
Straiten me on.   —I suffered living like a stain:

[34]
I trundle the bodies, on the iron bars,
over that fire backward & forth; they burn;
bits fall. I wonder if
I killed them. Women serve my turn.
—Dreams! You are good. —No. —Dense with hardihood
the wicked are dislodged, and lodged the good.
In green space we are safe.
God awaits us (but I   am yielding) who Hell wars.

[35]
—I cannot feel myself God waits. He flies
nearer a kindly world; or he is flown.
One Saturday's rescue
won't show. Man is entirely alone
may be. I am a man of griefs & fits
trying to be my friend. And the brown smock splits,
down the pale flesh a gash
broadens and Time holds up your heart against my eyes.

[36]

—Hard and divided heaven! creases me. Shame
is failing. My breath is scented, and I throw
hostile glances towards God.
Crumpling plunge of a pestle, bray:
sin cross & opposite, wherein I survive
nightmares of Eden. Reaches foul & live
he for me, this soul
to crunch, a minute tangle of eternal flame.

[37]

I fear Hell's hammer-wind. But fear does wane.
Death's blossoms grain my hair; I cannot live.
A black joy clashes
joy, in twilight. The Devil said
'I will deal toward her softly, and her enchanting cries
will fool the horns of Adam.' Father of lies,
a male great pestle smashes
small women swarming towards the mortar's rim in vain.

[38]

I see the cruel spread Wings black with saints!
Silky my breasts not his, mine, mine, to withhold
or tender, tender.
I am sifting, nervous, and bold.
The light is changing. Surrender this loveliness
you cannot make me do. *But* I will. Yes.
What horror, down stormy air,
warps towards me? My threatening promise faints—

[39]

torture me, Father, lest not I be thine!
Tribunal terrible & pure, my God,
mercy for him and me.
Faces half-fanged, Christ drives abroad,
and though the crop hopes, Jane is so slipshod
I cry. Evil dissolves, & love, like foam;

that love. Prattle of children powers me home,
my heart claps like the swan's
under a frenzy of *who* love me & who shine.

[40]

As a canoe slides by on one strong stroke
hope his hélp not I, who do hardly bear
his gift still. But whisper
I am not utterly. I pare
an apple for my pipsqueak Mercy and
she runs & all need naked apples, fanned
their tinier envies.
Vomitings, trots, rashes. Can be hope a cloak?

[41]

for the man with cropt ears glares. My fingers tighten
my skirt. I pass. Alas! I pity all.
Shy, shy, with mé, Dorothy.
Moonrise, and frightening hoots. 'Mother,
how *long* will I be dead?' Our friend the owl
vanishes, darling, but your homing soul
retires on Heaven, Mercy:
not we one instant die, only our dark does lighten.

[42]

When by me in the dusk my child sits down
I am myself. Simon, if it's that loose,
let me wiggle it out.
You'll get a bigger one there, & bite.
How they loft, how their sizes delight and grate.
The proportioned, spiritless poems accumulate.
And they publish them
away in brutish London, for a hollow crown.

[43]

Father is not himself. He keeps his bed,
and threw a saffron scum Thursday. God-forsaken words

escaped him raving. Save,
Lord, thy servant zealous & just.
Sam he saw back from Harvard. He did scold
his secting enemies. His stomach is cold
while we drip, while
my baby John breaks out. O far from where he bred!

[44]

Bone of moaning: sung Where he has gone
a thousand summers by truth-hallowed souls;
be still. Agh, he is gone!
Where? I know. Beyond the shoal.
Still–all a Christian daughter grinds her teeth
a little. This our land has ghosted with
our dead: I am at home.
Finish, Lord, in me this work thou hast begun.

[45]

And they tower, whom the pear-tree lured
to let them fall, fierce mornings they reclined
down the brook-bank to the east
fishing for shiners with a crookt pin,
wading, dams massing, well, and Sam's to be
a doctor in Boston. After the divisive sea,
and death's first feast,
and the galled effort on the wilderness endured,

[46]

Arminians, and the King bore against us;
of an 'inward light' we hear with horror.
Whose fan is in his hand
and he will throughly purge his floor,
come towards mé. I have what licks the joints
and bites the heart, which winter more appoints.
Iller I, oftener.
Hard at the outset; in the ending thus hard, thus?

[47]

Sacred & unutterable Mind
flashing thorough the universe one thought,
I do wait without peace.
In the article of death I budge.
Eat my sore breath, Black Angel. Let me die.
Body a-drain, when will you be dry
and countenance my speed
to Heaven's springs? lest stricter writhings have me declined.

[48]

'What are those pictures in the air at night,
Mother?' Mercy did ask. Space charged with faces
day & night! I place
a goatskin's fetor, and sweat: fold me
in savoury arms. Something is shaking, wrong.
He smells the musket and lifts it. It is long.
It points at my heart.
Missed he must have. In the gross storm of sunlight

[49]

I sniff a fire burning without outlet,
consuming acrid its own smoke. It's me.
Ruined laughter sounds
outside. Ah but I waken, free.
And so I am about again. I hagged
a fury at the short maid, whom tongues tagged,
and I am sorry. Once
less I was anxious when more passioned to upset

[50]

the mansion & the garden & the beauty of God.
Insectile unreflective busyness
blunts & does amend.
Hangnails, piles, fibs, life's also.
But we are that from which draws back a thumb.
The seasons stream and, somehow, I am become

an old woman. It's so:
I look. I bear to look. Strokes once more his rod.

[51]

My window gives on the graves, in our great new house
(how many burned?) upstairs, among the elms.
I lie, & endure, & wonder.
A haze slips sometimes over my dreams
and holiness on horses' bells shall stand.
Wandering pacemaker, unsteadying friend,
in a redskin calm I wait:
beat when you will our end. Sinkings & droopings drowse.

[52]

They say thro' the fading winter Dorothy fails,
my second, who than I bore one more, nine;
and I see her inearthed. I linger.
Seaborn she wed knelt before Simon;
Simon I, and linger. Black-yellow seething, vast
it lies fróm me, mine: all they look aghast.
It will be a glorious arm.
Docile I watch. My wreckt chest hurts when Simon pales.

[53]

In the yellowing days your faces wholly fail,
at Fall's onset. Solemn voices fade.
I feel no coverlet.
Light notes leap, a beckon, swaying
the tilted, sickening ear within. I'll—I'll—
I am closed & coming. Somewhere! I defile
wide as a cloud, in a cloud,
unfit, desirous, glad—even the singings veil—

[54]

—You are not ready? You áre ready. Pass,
as shadow gathers shadow in the welling night.
Fireflies of childhood torch

you down. We commit our sister down.
One candle mourn by, which a lover gave,
the use's edge and order of her grave.
Quiet? Moisture shoots.
Hungry throngs collect. They sword into the carcass.

[55]

Headstones stagger under great draughts of time
after heads pass out, and their world must reel
speechless, blind in the end
about its chilling star: thrift tuft,
whin cushion—nothing. Already with the wounded flying
dark air fills, I am a closet of secrets dying,
races murder, foxholes hold men,
reactor piles wage slow upon the wet brain rime.

[56]

I must pretend to leave you. Only you draw off
a benevolent phantom. I say you seem to me
drowned towns off England,
featureless as those myriads
who what bequeathed save fire-ash, fossils, burled
in the open river-drifts of the Old World?
Simon lived on for years.
I renounce not even ragged glances, small teeth, nothing,

[57]

O all your ages at the mercy of my loves
together lie at once, forever or
so long as I happen.
In the rain of pain & departure, still
Love has no body and presides the sun,
and elfs from silence melody. I run.
Hover, utter, still,
a sourcing   whom my lost candle like the firefly loves.

Stanzas

1–4   The poem is about the woman but this exordium is spoken by the poet, his voice modulating in stanza 4, line 8 [4.8] into hers.

1.1   He was not Governor until after her death.

1.5   Sylvester (the translator of Du Bartas) and Quarles, her favourite poets; unfortunately.

5.4,5   Many details are from quotations in Helen Campbell's biography, the Winthrop papers, narratives, town histories.

8.4ff.   Scriptural passages are sometimes ones she used herself, as this in her *Meditation liii*.

11.8   *that one:* the Old One.

12.5–13.2   The poet interrupts.

18.8   Her first child was not born until about 1633.

22.6   *chopping:* disputing, snapping, haggling; axing.

23.1   *fere:* his friend Death.

24.1   Her irony of 22.8 intensifies.

24.2   *rakes:* inclines, as a mast; bows.

25.3   One might say: He is enabled to speak, at last, in the fortune of an echo of her—and when she is loneliest (her former spiritual adviser having deserted Anne Hutchinson, and this her closest friend banished), as if she had summoned him; and only thus, perhaps, is she enabled to hear him. This second section of the poem is a dialogue, his voice however ceasing well before it ends at 39.4, and hers continuing for the whole third part, until the coda (54–57).

29.1–4   Cf. Isa. 1:5.

29.5,6   After a Klee.

33.1   Cf., on Byzantine icons, Frederick Rolfe ('Baron Corvo'): 'Who ever dreams of praying (with expectation of response) for the prayer of a Tintoretto or a Titian, or a Bellini, or a Botticelli? But who can refrain from crying "O Mother!" to these unruffleable wan dolls in indigo on gold?' (quoted from *The Desire and Pursuit of the Whole* by Graham Greene in *The Lost Childhood*).

33.5,6   'Délires des grandes profondeurs,' described by Cousteau and others; a euphoria, sometimes fatal, in which the hallucinated diver offers passing fish his line, helmet, anything.

35.3,4 As of cliffhangers, movie serials wherein each week's episode ends with a train bearing down on the strapped heroine or with the hero dangling over an abyss into which Indians above him peer with satisfaction before they hatchet the rope. *rescue:* forcible recovery (by the owner) of goods distrained.

37.7,8 After an engraving somewhere in Fuchs's collections. *Bray,* above (36.4), puns.

39.5 The stanza is unsettled, like 24, by a middle line, signaling a broad transition.

42.8 *brutish:* her epithet for London in a kindly passage about the Great Fire.

46.1,2 Arminians, rebels against the doctrine of unconditional election. Her husband alone opposed the law condemning Quakers to death.

46.3,4 Matthew 3:12.

46.5,6 Rheumatic fever, after a celebrated French description.

48.2ff. *Space . . . outside:* delirium.

51.5 Cf. Zech. 14:20.

51.6 *Wandering pacemaker:* a disease of the heart, here the heart itself.

52.4 Seaborn Cotton, John's eldest son; Bradstreet being then magistrate.

52.5,6 Dropsical, a complication of the last three years. Line 7 she actually said.

55.4 *thrift:* the plant, also called Our Lady's cushion.

55.8 *wet brain:* edema.

56.5,6 Cf. G. R. Levy, *The Gate of Horn,* p. 5.

A Sympathy, A Welcome

Feel for your bad fall how could I fail,
poor Paul, who had it so good.
I can offer you only: this world like a knife.
Yet you'll get to know your mother
and humourless as you do look you will laugh
and all the others
will NOT be fierce to you, and loverhood
will swing your soul like a broken bell

deep in a forsaken wood, poor Paul,
whose wild bad father loves you well.

OF SUICIDE

Reflexions on suicide, & on my father, possess me.
I drink too much. My wife threatens separation.
She won't 'nurse' me. She feels 'inadequate'.
We don't mix together.

It's an hour later in the East.
I could call up Mother in Washington, D.C.
But could she help me?
And all this postal adulation & reproach?

A basis rock-like of love & friendship
for all this world-wide madness seems to be needed.
Epictetus is in some ways my favourite philosopher.
Happy men have died earlier.

I still plan to go to Mexico this summer.
The Olmec images! Chichén Itzá!
D. H. Lawrence has a wild dream of it.
Malcolm Lowry's book when it came out I taught to my
    precept at Princeton.

I don't entirely resign. I may teach the Third Gospel
this afternoon. I haven't made up my mind.
It seems to me sometimes that others have easier jobs
& do them worse.

Well, we must labour & dream. Gogol was impotent,
somebody in Pittsburgh told me.
I said: At what age? They couldn't answer.
That is a damned serious matter.

Rembrandt was sober. There we differ. Sober.
Terrors came on him. To us too they come.
Of suicide I continually think.
Apparently he didn't. I'll teach Luke.

DEATH BALLAD

('I don't care')

Tyson & Jo, Tyson & Jo
became convinced it was no go
& decided to end it all
at nineteen,—on the psychiatric ward.

Trouble is, Tyson was on the locked ward,
Jo for some reason on the open
and they were forbidden to communicate
either their love or their hate.

Heroin & the cops were Tyson's bit
I don't know just what Jo's was, ah but it
was more self-destructive still.
She tried to tear a window & screen out.

United in their feel of worthlessness
& rage, they stood like sisters in their way
blocking their path. They made a list
of the lies of Society & glared: 'We don't exist.'

The charismatic quality of these charming & sensitive girls
smiled thro' their vices; all were fond of them
& wished them well.
They sneered: 'We prefer Hell.'

What will their fates be? Put their heads together,
in their present mental weather,
no power can prevent their dying. That is so.
Only, Jo & Tyson, Tyson & Jo,

take up, outside your blocked selves, some small thing
that is moving
& wants to keep on moving
& needs therefore, Tyson, Jo, your loving.

He Resigns

Age, and the deaths, and the ghosts.
Her having gone away
in spirit from me. Hosts
of regrets come & find me empty.

I don't feel this will change.
I don't want any thing
or person, familiar or strange.
I don't think I will sing

any more just now;
ever. I must start
to sit with a blind brow
above an empty heart.

Henry By Night

Henry's nocturnal habits were the terror of his women.
First it appears he snored, lying on his back.
Then he thrashed & tossed,
changing position like a task fleet. Then, inhuman,
he woke every hour or so—they couldn't keep track
of mobile Henry, lost

at 3 a.m., off for more drugs or a cigarette,
reading old mail, writing new letters, scribbling
excessive Songs;
back then to bed, to the old tune or get set

for a stercoraceous cough, without quibbling
death-like. His women's wrongs

they hoarded & forgave, mysterious, sweet;
but you'll admit it was no way to live
or even keep alive.
I won't mention the dreams I won't repeat
sweating & shaking: something's gotta give:
up for good at five.

Henry's Understanding

He was reading late, at Richard's, down in Maine,
aged 32? Richard & Helen long in bed,
my good wife long in bed.
All I had to do was strip & get into my bed,
putting the marker in the book, & sleep,
& wake to a hot breakfast.

Off the coast was an island, P'tit Manaan,
the bluff from Richard's lawn was almost sheer.
A chill at four o'clock.
It only takes a few minutes to make a man.
A concentration upon now & here.
Suddenly, unlike Bach,

& horribly, unlike Bach, it occurred to me
that *one* night, instead of warm pajamas,
I'd take off all my clothes
& cross the damp cold lawn & down the bluff
into the terrible water & walk forever
under it out toward the island.

EPILOGUE

He died in December. He must descend
Somewhere, vague and cold, the spirit and seal,
The gift descend, and all that insight fail
Somewhere. Imagination one's one friend
Cannot see there. Both of us at the end.
Nouns, verbs do not exist for what I feel.

THE DREAM SONGS

1

Huffy Henry hid   the day,
unappeasable Henry sulked.
I see his point,—a trying to put things over.
It was the thought that they thought
they could *do* it made Henry wicked & away.
But he should have come out and talked.

All the world like a woolen lover
once did seem on Henry's side.
Then came a departure.
Thereafter nothing fell out as it might or ought.
I don't see how Henry, pried
open for all the world to see, survived.

What he has now to say is a long
wonder the world can bear & be.
Once in a sycamore I was glad
all at the top, and I sang.
Hard on the land wears the strong sea
and empty grows every bed.

4

Filling her compact & delicious body
with chicken páprika, she glanced at me
twice.
Fainting with interest, I hungered back
and only the fact of her husband & four other people
kept me from springing on her

or falling at her little feet and crying
'You are the hottest one for years of night
Henry's dazed eyes
have enjoyed, Brilliance.' I advanced upon
(despairing) my spumoni.—Sir Bones: is stuffed,
de world, wif feeding girls.

—Black hair, complexion Latin, jewelled eyes
downcast . . . The slob beside her   feasts . . . What wonders
     is
she sitting on, over there?
The restaurant buzzes. She might as well be on Mars.
Where did it all go wrong? There ought to be a law against
     Henry.
—Mr. Bones: there is.

14

Life, friends, is boring. We must not say so.
After all, the sky flashes, the great sea yearns,
we ourselves flash and yearn,
and moreover my mother told me as a boy
(repeatingly) 'Ever to confess you're bored
means you have no

Inner Resources.' I conclude now I have no
inner resources, because I am heavy bored.
Peoples bore me,
literature bores me, especially great literature,
Henry bores me, with his plights & gripes
as bad as achilles,

who loves people and valiant art, which bores me.
And the tranquil hills, & gin, look like a drag
and somehow a dog
has taken itself & its tail considerably away
into mountains or sea or sky, leaving
behind: me, wag.

18

A STRUT FOR ROETHKE

Westward, hit a low note, for a roarer lost
across the Sound but north from Bremerton,
hit a way down note.
And never cadenza again of flowers, or cost.
Him who could really do that cleared his throat
& staggered on.

The bluebells, pool-shallows, saluted his over-needs,
while the clouds growled, heh-heh, & snapped, & crashed.

No stunt he'll ever unflinch once more will fail
(O lucky fellow, eh Bones?)—drifted off upstairs,
downstairs, somewheres.
No more daily, trying to hit the head on the nail:
thirstless: without a think in his head:
back from wherever, with it said.

Hit a high long note, for a lover found
needing a lower into friendlier ground
to bug among worms no more
around um jungles where ah blurt 'What for?'
Weeds, too, he favoured as   most men don't favour men.
The Garden Master's gone.

The glories of the world struck me, made me aria, once.
—What happen then, Mr Bones?
if be you cares to say.
—Henry. Henry became interested in women's bodies,
his loins were & were the   scene of stupendous achievement.
Stupor. Knees, dear. Pray.

All the knobs & softnesses of, my God,
the ducking & trouble it swarm on Henry,
at one time.
—What happen then, Mr Bones?
you seems excited-like.
—Fell Henry back into   the original crime: art, rime

besides a sense of others, my God, my God,
and a jealousy for the honour (alive) of his country,
what can get more odd?
and discontent with the thriving gangs & pride.
—What happen then, Mr Bones?
—I had a most marvellous   piece of luck. I died.

There sat down, once, a thing on Henry's heart
só heavy, if he had a hundred years
& more, & weeping, sleepless, in all them time
Henry could not make good.
Starts again always in Henry's ears
the little cough somewhere, an odour, a chime.

And there is another thing he has in mind
like a grave Sienese face a thousand years
would fail to blur the still profiled reproach of. Ghastly,
with open eyes, he attends, blind.
All the bells say: too late. This is not for tears;
thinking.

But never did Henry, as he thought he did,
end anyone and hacks her body up
and hide the pieces, where they may be found.
He knows: he went over everyone, & nobody's missing.
Often he reckons, in the dawn, them up.
Nobody is ever missing.

35

MLA

Hey, out there!—assistant professors, full,
associates,—instructors—others—any—
I have a sing to shay.
We are assembled here in the capital
city for Dull—and one professor's wife is Mary—
at Christmastide, hey!

and all of you did theses or are doing
and the moral history of what we were up to
thrives in Sir Wilson's hands—
who I don't see here—only deals go screwing
some of you out, some up—the chairmen too
are nervous, little friends—

a chairman's not a chairman, son, forever,
and hurts with his appointments; ha, but circle—
take my word for it—
though maybe Frost is dying—around Mary;
forget your footnotes on the old gentleman;
dance around Mary.

40

I'm scared a lonely. Never see my son,
easy be not to see anyone,
combers out to sea
know they're goin somewhere but not me.

Got a little poison, got a little gun,
I'm scared a lonely.

I'm scared a only one thing, which is me,
from othering I don't take nothin, see,
for any hound dog's sake.
But this is where I livin, where I rake
my leaves and cop my promise, this' where we
cry oursel's awake.

Wishin was dyin but I gotta make
it all this way to that bed on these feet
where peoples said to meet.
Maybe but even if I see my son
forever never, get back on the take,
free, black & forty-one.

75

Turning it over, considering, like a madman
Henry put forth a book.
No harm resulted from this.
Neither the menstruating   stars (nor man) was moved
at once.
Bare dogs drew closer for a second look

and performed their friendly operations there.
Refreshed, the bark rejoiced.
Seasons went and came.
Leaves fell, but only a few.
Something remarkable about this
unshedding bulky bole-proud blue-green moist

thing made by savage & thoughtful
surviving Henry
began to strike the passers from despair
so that sore on their shoulders old men hoisted
six-foot sons and polished women called

small girls to dream awhile toward the flashing & bursting
tree!

76

HENRY'S CONFESSION

Nothin very bad happen to me lately.
How you explain that?—I explain that, Mr Bones,
terms o' your bafflin odd sobriety.
Sober as man can get, no girls, no telephones,
what could happen bad to Mr Bones?
—*If* life is a handkerchief sandwich,

in a modesty of death I join my father
who dared so long agone leave me.
A bullet on a concrete stoop
close by a smothering southern sea
spreadeagled on an island, by my knee.
—You is from hunger, Mr Bones,

I offers you this handkerchief, now set
your left foot by my right foot,
shoulder to shoulder, all that jazz,
arm in arm, by the beautiful sea,
hum a little, Mr Bones.
—I saw nobody coming, so I went instead.

77

Seedy Henry rose up shy in de world
& shaved & swung his barbells, duded Henry up
and p.a.'d poor thousands of persons on topics of grand
moment to Henry, ah to those less & none.
Wif a book of his in either hand
he is stript down to move on.

—Come away, Mr Bones.

—Henry is tired of the winter,
& haircuts, & a squeamish comfy   ruin-prone proud national
    mind,   & Spring (in the city so called).
Henry likes Fall.
Hé would be prepared to líve in a world of Fáll
for ever, impenitent Henry.
But the snows and summers grieve & dream;

thése fierce & airy occupations, and love,
raved away so many of Henry's years
it is a wonder that, with in each hand
one of his own mad books and all,
ancient fires for eyes, his head full
& his heart full, he's making ready to move on.

134

Sick at 6 & sick again at 9
was Henry's gloomy Monday morning oh.
Still he had to lecture.
They waited, his little children, for stricken Henry
to rise up yet once more again and come oh.
They figured he was a fixture,

nuts to their bolts, keys to their bloody locks.
One day the whole affair will fall apart
with a rustle of fire,
a wrestle of undoing, as of tossed clocks,
and somewhere not far off a broken heart
for hire.

He had smoked a pack of cigarettes by 10
& was ready to go. Peace to his ashes then,
poor Henry,
with all this gas & shit blowing through it
four times in 2 hours, his tail ached.
He arose, benign, & performed.

149

This world is gradually becoming a place
where I do not care to be any more. Can Delmore die?
I don't suppose
in all them years a day went ever by
without a loving thought for him. Welladay.
In the brightness of his promise,

unstained, I saw him thro' the mist of the actual
blazing with insight, warm with gossip
thro' all our Harvard years
when both of us were just becoming known
I got him out of a police-station once, in Washington, the
    world is *tref*
and grief too astray for tears.

I imagine you have heard the terrible news,
that Delmore Schwartz is dead, miserably & alone,
in New York: he sang me a song
'I am the Brooklyn poet Delmore Schwartz
Harms & the child I sing, two parents' torts'
when he was young & gift-strong.

153

I'm cross with god who has wrecked this generation.
First he seized Ted, then Richard, Randall, and now
    Delmore.
In between he gorged on Sylvia Plath.
That was a first rate haul. He left alive
fools I could number like a kitchen knife
but Lowell he did not touch.

Somewhere the enterprise continues, not—
yellow the sun lies on the baby's blouse—
in Henry's staggered thought.
I suppose the word would be, we must submit.
Later.
I hang, and I will not be part of it.

A friend of Henry's contrasted God's career
with Mozart's, leaving Henry with nothing to say
but praise for a word so apt.
We suffer on, a day, a day, a day.
And never again can come, like a man slapped,
news like this

187

Them lady poets must not marry, pal.
Miss Dickinson—fancy in Amherst bedding hér.
Fancy a lark with Sappho,
a tumble in the bushes with Miss Moore,
a spoon with Emily, while Charlotte glare.
Miss Bishop's too noble-O.

That was the lot. And two of them are here
as yet, and—and: Sylvia Plath is not.
She—she her credentials
has handed in, leaving alone two tots
and widower to what he makes of it—
surviving guy, &

when Tolstoy's pathetic widow doing her whung
(after them decades of marriage) & kids, she decided he
 was *queer*
& loving his agent.
Wherefore he rush off, leaving two journals, & die.
It is a true error to marry with poets
or to be by them.

235

Tears Henry shed for poor old Hemingway
Hemingway in despair, Hemingway at the end,
the end of Hemingway,
tears in a diningroom in Indiana
and that was years ago, before his marriage say,
God to him no worse luck send.

Save us from shotguns & fathers' suicides.
It all depends on who you're the father *of*
if you want to kill yourself—
a bad example, murder of oneself,
the final death, in a paroxysm, of love
for which good mercy hides?

A girl at the door: 'A few coppers pray'
But to return, to return to Hemingway
that cruel & gifted man.
Mercy! my father; do not pull the trigger
or all my life I'll suffer from your anger
killing what you began.

236

When Henry swung, in that great open square,
the crowd was immense, the little clouds were white
and it was all well done.
It's true he did it, because more to bear
of her open eyes & mute mouth at midnight
behind her little counter

by the others mangled, trying on her throat
with a lard knife: he took his shoemaker's
and it was all well done.
For more to bear he could, ha he could not
with a lard knife. His guilty thought had had takers
and here they were at it.

And the rest got off & somehow here he swings
in the open air of an Edinburgh morning
for an impulse of mercy.
Who's good, who's evil, whose tail or whose wings
crosses his failing mind. The stop was mourning
and it was all well done.

An Elegy for *W.C.W.*, the lovely man

Henry in Ireland to Bill underground:
Rest well, who worked so hard, who made a good sound
constantly, for so many years:
your high-jinks delighted the continents & our ears:
you had so many girls your life was a triumph
and you loved your one wife.

At dawn you rose & wrote—the books poured forth—
you delivered infinite babies, in one great birth—
and your generosity
to juniors made you deeply loved, deeply:
if envy was a Henry trademark, he would envy you,
especially the being through.

Too many journeys lie for him ahead,
too many galleys & page-proofs to be read,
he would like to lie down
in your sweet silence, to whom was not denied
the mysterious late excellence which is the crown
of our trials & our last bride.

382

At Henry's bier let some thing fall out well:
enter there none who somewhat has to sell,
the music ancient & gradual,
the voices solemn but the grief subdued,
no hairy jokes but everybody's mood
subdued, subdued,

until the Dancer comes, in a short short dress
hair black & long & loose, dark dark glasses,
uptilted face,

pallor & strangeness, the music changes
to 'Give!' & 'Ow!' and how! the music changes,
she kicks a backward limb

on tiptoe, pirouettes, & she is free
to the knocking music, sails, dips, & suddenly
returns to the terrible gay
occasion hopeless & mad, she weaves, it's hell,
she flings to her head a leg, bobs, all is well,
she dances Henry away.

384

The marker slants, flowerless, day's almost done,
I stand above my father's grave with rage,
often, often before
I've made this awful pilgrimage to one
who cannot visit me, who tore his page
out: I come back for more,

I spit upon this dreadful banker's grave
who shot his heart out in a Florida dawn
O ho alas alas
When will indifference come, I moan & rave
I'd like to scrabble till I got right down
away down under the grass

and ax the casket open ha to see
just how he's taking it, which he sought so hard
we'll tear apart
the mouldering grave clothes ha & then Henry
will heft the ax once more, his final card,
and fell it on the start.

My daughter's heavier. Light leaves are flying.
Everywhere in enormous numbers turkeys will be dying
and other birds, all their wings.
They never greatly flew. Did they wish to?
I should know. Off away somewhere once I knew
such things.

Or good Ralph Hodgson back then did, or does.
The man is dead whom Eliot praised. My praise
follows and flows too late.
Fall is grievy, brisk. Tears behind the eyes
almost fall. Fall comes to us as a prize
to rouse us toward our fate.

My house is made of wood and it's made well,
unlike us. My house is older than Henry;
that's fairly old.
If there were a middle   ground between things and the soul
or if the sky resembled more the sea,
I wouldn't have to scold

                                        my heavy

    daughter.

ANNE SEXTON

institutionalized for nightmarish depressions or for suicidal drug overdoses. Finally, shortly before her forty-sixth birthday, she succeeded in taking her life, possibly as a way of avoiding almost inevitable permanent incarceration. Wrapped in her mother's fur coat, her affairs having been put neatly in order, she sat in her car in a closed garage with the motor idling.

It is remarkable, given her often-paralyzing symptoms, not only that Sexton was so productive (one entire book, *The Awful Rowing toward God,* was composed in less than three weeks) but that she was able to perform memorably at public readings, both solo and with a small rock group called "Anne Sexton and Her Kind," which accompanied her poems with music. (Those unimpressed by her exhibitionism tended to dismiss her as the Janis Joplin of the poetry-reading circuit. Partly because of her flamboyant public image and partly because her work was both accessible and popular, she has not received unqualified approval from the academic establishment.) Like actors who can step out of themselves to inhabit a dramatic role, Sexton was capable of shedding her pre-performance anxieties and of presenting a vivid, confident persona to her audiences. I heard her read just once, in Philadelphia, and was struck not only by the terrible beauty of the poetry but by her electric presence, self-effacing humor, and utterly unembarrassed narcissism. (I was reminded of William James's description of his sister Alice—"bottled lightning.") Clearly a born performer, she often took days to recover from one of these intense appearances.

At her readings she liked to quote Kafka's observation that "a book should serve as the ax for the frozen sea within us." Her own unabashedly therapeutic writing was initiated by her psychiatrist, Martin Orne, who felt that it would not only provide an outlet for her pain and confusion, thus enhancing her self-esteem, but serve to inspire others suffering from mental disorders. Unlike the rest of the artists in this anthology, Sexton had virtually no formal education in literary history (a fact that contributed to her sense of unworthiness); the poet James Wright once commented that a conversation with her was like hearing Emily Dickinson apologize for a mistake in punctuation.

Guided, however, by her mentors, especially Robert Lowell, she quickly developed the ability to compose instinctively within organized, received structures without sacrificing the uninhibited, crude power ("I hold back nothing") that distinguishes her best work. She was able, again like Lowell, to harness her compulsiveness into productive if exhaustive fine-tuning of what she had written.

Sexton was influenced by W. D. Snodgrass's *Heart's Needle,* poetry that deals candidly with the intimate details of his divorce and its effect on his relationship with his young daughter. The book, arguably the first in the confessional mode, gave her the courage (or "permission," as she put it) to mine her own troubled autobiography for taboo material that, however artistically organized, went well beyond the usual boundaries imposed by decorum and tradition. As her closest friend, the poet Maxine Kumin, has said, Sexton "wrote openly about menstruation, abortion, masturbation, incest, adultery, and drug addiction at a time when the proprieties embraced none of these as proper topics for poetry. . . . Anne delineated the problematic position of women—the neurotic reality of the time—though she was not able to cope in her own life with the personal trouble it created."

> Sleepmonger,
> deathmonger,
> with capsules in my palms each night,
> eight at a time from sweet pharmaceutical bottles
> I make arrangements for a pint-sized journey.
> I am the queen of this condition.
> I'm an expert on making the trip
> And now they say I'm an addict.
> Now they ask why.
> Why!
>
> from "The Addict"

When an interviewer asked Joyce Carol Oates in 1969 what she would like to see placed in a time capsule on the moon, she responded, "The confessional poetry of Anne Sexton, Sylvia Plath, Robert Lowell, and W. D. Snodgrass." For her part, Sexton saw herself as "the only confessional poet," the one who went farthest in exorcising her private demons by "writing from the unconscious" and in exploring through a poetics of free association the morbid, decidedly unpoetic roots of her self-hatred and madness. Her work clearly embodies the characteristics Lowell had in mind when he distinguished between poetry that is "raw" as opposed to "cooked": the latter, "marvelously expert and remote, seems constructed . . . for graduate seminars," while the raw is "jerry-built and forensically deadly."

Sexton, who liked to describe herself as a witch ("mouth wide, / ready to tell you a story or two"), said she wanted "to scare people," certainly one of the things her forensically deadly art does. But whether such work is "confessional" or "raw" or "exhibitionistic" can be left for critics to debate. What is unarguable is that her provocative, dangerous verse, especially in the more formally organized early books, where compression and verbal wit predominate, has a permanent place in the American poetic canon. In James Wright's words, "any history of American literature which failed to include a long and careful discussion of her works would be critically and historically incomplete."

The Complete Poems (Houghton Mifflin Company, 1982). Diane Wood Middlebrook, *Anne Sexton: A Biography* (Houghton Mifflin, 1991). For criticism, see *Anne Sexton: The Artist and Her Critics,* edited by J. D. McClatchy (Indiana University Press, 1978).

MUSIC SWIMS BACK TO ME

Wait Mister. Which way is home?
They turned the light out
and the dark is moving in the corner.

There are no sign posts in this room,
four ladies, over eighty,
in diapers every one of them.
La la la, Oh music swims back to me
and I can feel the tune they played
the night they left me
in this private institution on a hill.

Imagine it. A radio playing
and everyone here was crazy.
I liked it and danced in a circle.
Music pours over the sense
and in a funny way
music sees more than I.
I mean it remembers better;
remembers the first night here.
It was the strangled cold of November;
even the stars were strapped in the sky
and that moon too bright
forking through the bars to stick me
with a singing in the head.
I have forgotten all the rest.

They lock me in this chair at eight a.m.
and there are no signs to tell the way,
just the radio beating to itself
and the song that remembers
more than I. Oh, la la la,
this music swims back to me.
The night I came I danced a circle
and was not afraid.
Mister?

as again tonight he'll say
honey bunch let's go
and she will not say how there
must be more to living
than this brief bright bridge
of the raucous bed or even
the slow braille touch of him
like a heavy god grown light,
that old pantomime of love
that she wants although
it leaves her still alone,
built back again at last,
mind's apart from him, living
her own self in her own words
and hating the sweat of the house
they keep when they finally lie
each in separate dreams
and then how she watches him,
still strong in the blowzy bag
of his usual sleep while
her young years bungle past
their same marriage bed
and she wishes him cripple, or poet,
or even lonely, or sometimes,
better, my lover, dead.

RINGING THE BELLS

And this is the way they ring
the bells in Bedlam
and this is the bell-lady
who comes each Tuesday morning
to give us a music lesson
and because the attendants make you go
and because we mind by instinct,
like bees caught in the wrong hive,

we are the circle of the crazy ladies
who sit in the lounge of the mental house
and smile at the smiling woman
who passes us each a bell,
who points at my hand
that holds my bell, E flat,
and this is the gray dress next to me
who grumbles as if it were special
to be old, to be old,
and this is the small hunched squirrel girl
on the other side of me
who picks at the hairs over her lip,
who picks at the hairs over her lip all day,
and this is how the bells really sound,
as untroubled and clean
as a workable kitchen,
and this is always my bell responding
to my hand that responds to the lady
who points at me, E flat;
and although we are no better for it,
they tell you to go. And you do.

ELEGY IN THE CLASSROOM

In the thin classroom, where your face
was noble and your words were all things,
I find this boily creature in your place;

find you disarranged, squatting on the window sill,
irrefutably placed up there,
like a hunk of some big frog
watching us through the V
of your woolen legs.

Even so, I must admire your skill.
You are so gracefully insane.

We fidget in our plain chairs
and pretend to catalogue
our facts for your burly sorcery

or ignore your fat blind eyes
or the prince you ate yesterday
who was wise, wise, wise.

THE TRUTH THE DEAD KNOW

FOR MY MOTHER, BORN MARCH 1902, DIED MARCH 1959
AND MY FATHER, BORN FEBRUARY 1900, DIED JUNE 1959

Gone, I say and walk from church,
refusing the stiff procession to the grave,
letting the dead ride alone in the hearse.
It is June. I am tired of being brave.

We drive to the Cape. I cultivate
myself where the sun gutters from the sky,
where the sea swings in like an iron gate
and we touch. In another country people die.

My darling, the wind falls in like stones
from the whitehearted water and when we touch
we enter touch entirely. No one's alone.
Men kill for this, or for as much.

And what of the dead? They lie without shoes
in their stone boats. They are more like stone
than the sea would be if it stopped. They refuse
to be blessed, throat, eye and knucklebone.

Young

A thousand doors ago
when I was a lonely kid
in a big house with four
garages and it was summer
as long as I could remember,
I lay on the lawn at night,
clover wrinkling under me,
the wise stars bedding over me,
my mother's window a funnel
of yellow heat running out,
my father's window, half shut,
an eye where sleepers pass,
and the boards of the house
were smooth and white as wax
and probably a million leaves
sailed on their strange stalks
as the crickets ticked together
and I, in my brand new body,
which was not a woman's yet,
told the stars my questions
and thought God could really see
the heat and the painted light,
elbows, knees, dreams, goodnight.

The Starry Night

That does not keep me from having a terrible need of—shall I say the word—religion. Then I go out at night to paint the stars.
—Vincent Van Gogh in a letter to his brother

The town does not exist
except where one black-haired tree slips
up like a drowned woman into the hot sky.
The town is silent. The night boils with eleven stars.

Oh starry starry night! This is how
I want to die.

It moves. They are all alive.
Even the moon bulges in its orange irons
to push children, like a god, from its eye.
The old unseen serpent swallows up the stars.
Oh starry starry night! This is how
I want to die:

into that rushing beast of the night,
sucked up by that great dragon, to split
from my life with no flag,
no belly,
no cry.

LITTLE GIRL, MY STRING BEAN,
MY LOVELY WOMAN

My daughter, at eleven
(almost twelve), is like a garden.

Oh, darling! Born in that sweet birthday suit
and having owned it and known it for so long,
now you must watch high noon enter—
noon, that ghost hour.
Oh, funny little girl—this one under a blueberry sky,
this one! How can I say that I've known
just what you know and just where you are?

It's not a strange place, this odd home
where your face sits in my hand
so full of distance,
so full of its immediate fever.
The summer has seized you,

as when, last month in Amalfi, I saw
lemons as large as your desk-side globe—
that miniature map of the world—
and I could mention, too,
the market stalls of mushrooms
and garlic buds all engorged.
Or I think even of the orchard next door,
where the berries are done
and the apples are beginning to swell.
And once, with our first backyard,
I remember I planted an acre of yellow beans
we couldn't eat.

Oh, little girl,
my stringbean,
how do you grow?
You grow this way.
You are too many to eat.

I hear
as in a dream
the conversation of the old wives
speaking of *womanhood.*
I remember that I heard nothing myself.
I was alone.
I waited like a target.

Let high noon enter—
the hour of the ghosts.
Once the Romans believed
that noon was the ghost hour,
and I can believe it, too,
under that startling sun,
and someday they will come to you,
someday, men bare to the waist, young Romans
at noon where they belong,

with ladders and hammers
while no one sleeps.

But before they enter
I will have said,
Your bones are lovely,
and before their strange hands
there was always this hand that formed.

Oh, darling, let your body in,
let it tie you in,
in comfort.
What I want to say, Linda,
is that women are born twice.

If I could have watched you grow
as a magical mother might,
if I could have seen through my magical transparent belly,
there would have been such ripening within:
your embryo,
the seed taking on its own,
life clapping the bedpost,
bones from the pond,
thumbs and two mysterious eyes,
the awfully human head,
the heart jumping like a puppy,
the important lungs,
the becoming—
while it becomes!
as it does now,
a world of its own,
a delicate place.

I say hello
to such shakes and knockings and high jinks,
such music, such sprouts,

such dancing-mad-bears of music,
such necessary sugar,
such goings-on!

Oh, little girl,
my stringbean,
how do you grow?
You grow this way.
You are too many to eat.

What I want to say, Linda,
is that there is nothing in your body that lies.
All that is new is telling the truth.
I'm here, that somebody else,
an old tree in the background.

Darling,
stand still at your door,
sure of yourself, a white stone, a good stone—
as exceptional as laughter
you will strike fire,
that new thing!

PAIN FOR A DAUGHTER

Blind with love, my daughter
has cried nightly for horses,
those long-necked marchers and churners
that she has mastered, any and all,
reining them in like a circus hand—
the excitable muscles and the ripe neck;
tending this summer, a pony and a foal.
She who is too squeamish to pull
a thorn from the dog's paw,
watched her pony blossom with distemper,
the underside of the jaw swelling

like an enormous grape.
Gritting her teeth with love,
she drained the boil and scoured it
with hydrogen peroxide until pus
ran like milk on the barn floor.

Blind with loss all winter,
in dungarees, a ski jacket and a hard hat,
she visits the neighbors' stable,
our acreage not zoned for barns;
they who own the flaming horses
and the swan-whipped thoroughbred
that she tugs at and cajoles,
thinking it will burn like a furnace
under her small-hipped English seat.

Blind with pain she limps home.
The thoroughbred has stood on her foot.
He rested there like a building.
He grew into her foot until they were one.
The marks of the horseshoe printed
into her flesh, the tips of her toes
ripped off like pieces of leather,
three toenails swirled like shells
and left to float in blood in her riding boot.

Blind with fear, she sits on the toilet,
her foot balanced over the washbasin,
her father, hydrogen peroxide in hand,
performing the rites of the cleansing.
She bites on a towel, sucked in breath,
sucked in and arched against the pain,
her eyes glancing off me where
I stand at the door, eyes locked
on the ceiling, eyes of a stranger,
and then she cries . . .
Oh my God, help me!

Where a child would have cried *Mama!*
Where a child would have believed *Mama!*
she bit the towel and called on God
and I saw her life stretch out . . .
I saw her torn in childbirth,
and I saw her, at that moment,
in her own death and I knew that she
knew.

THE TOUCH

For months my hand had been sealed off
in a tin box. Nothing was there but subway railings.
Perhaps it is bruised, I thought,
and that is why they have locked it up.
But when I looked in it lay there quietly.
You could tell time by this, I thought,
like a clock, by its five knuckles
and the thin underground veins.
It lay there like an unconscious woman
fed by tubes she knew not of.

The hand had collapsed,
a small wood pigeon
that had gone into seclusion.
I turned it over and the palm was old,
its lines traced like fine needlepoint
and stitched up into the fingers.
It was fat and soft and blind in places.
Nothing but vulnerable.

And all this is metaphor.
An ordinary hand—just lonely
for something to touch
that touches back.
The dog won't do it.

Her tail wags in the swamp for a frog.
I'm no better than a case of dog food.
She owns her own hunger.
My sisters won't do it.
They live in school except for buttons
and tears running down like lemonade.
My father won't do it.
He comes with the house and even at night
he lives in a machine made by my mother
and well oiled by his job, his job.
The trouble is
that I'd let my gestures freeze.
The trouble was not
in the kitchen or the tulips
but only in my head, my head.

Then all this became history.
Your hand found mine.
Life rushed to my fingers like a blood clot.
Oh, my carpenter,
the fingers are rebuilt.
They dance with yours.
They dance in the attic and in Vienna.
My hand is alive all over America.
Not even death will stop it,
death shedding her blood.
Nothing will stop it, for this is the kingdom
and the kingdom come.

Snow White and the Seven Dwarfs

No matter what life you lead
the virgin is a lovely number:
cheeks as fragile as cigarette paper,
arms and legs made of Limoges,
lips like Vin Du Rhône,

rolling her china-blue doll eyes
open and shut.
Open to say,
Good Day Mama,
and shut for the thrust
of the unicorn.
She is unsoiled.
She is as white as a bonefish.

Once there was a lovely virgin
called Snow White.
Say she was thirteen.
Her stepmother,
a beauty in her own right,
though eaten, of course, by age,
would hear of no beauty surpassing her own.
Beauty is a simple passion,
but, oh my friends, in the end
you will dance the fire dance in iron shoes.
The stepmother had a mirror to which she referred—
something like the weather forecast—
a mirror that proclaimed
the one beauty of the land.
She would ask,
Looking glass upon the wall,
who is fairest of us all?
And the mirror would reply,
You are fairest of us all.
Pride pumped in her like poison.

Suddenly one day the mirror replied,
Queen, you are full fair, 'tis true,
but Snow White is fairer than you.
Until that moment Snow White
had been no more important
than a dust mouse under the bed.
But now the queen saw brown spots on her hand

and four whiskers over her lip
so she condemned Snow White
to be hacked to death.
Bring me her heart, she said to the hunter,
and I will salt it and eat it.
The hunter, however, let his prisoner go
and brought a boar's heart back to the castle.
The queen chewed it up like a cube steak.
Now I am fairest, she said,
lapping her slim white fingers.

Snow White walked in the wildwood
for weeks and weeks.
At each turn there were twenty doorways
and at each stood a hungry wolf,
his tongue lolling out like a worm.
The birds called out lewdly,
talking like pink parrots,
and the snakes hung down in loops,
each a noose for her sweet white neck.
On the seventh week
she came to the seventh mountain
and there she found the dwarf house.
It was as droll as a honeymoon cottage
and completely equipped with
seven beds, seven chairs, seven forks
and seven chamber pots.
Snow White ate seven chicken livers
and lay down, at last, to sleep.

The dwarfs, those little hot dogs,
walked three times around Snow White,
the sleeping virgin. They were wise
and wattled like small czars.
Yes. It's a good omen,
they said, and will bring us luck.
They stood on tiptoes to watch

Snow White wake up. She told them
about the mirror and the killer-queen
and they asked her to stay and keep house.
Beware of your stepmother,
they said.
Soon she will know you are here.
While we are away in the mines
during the day, you must not
open the door.

Looking glass upon the wall . . .
The mirror told
and so the queen dressed herself in rags
and went out like a peddler to trap Snow White.
She went across seven mountains.
She came to the dwarf house
and Snow White opened the door
and bought a bit of lacing.
The queen fastened it tightly
around her bodice,
as tight as an Ace bandage,
so tight that Snow White swooned.
She lay on the floor, a plucked daisy.
When the dwarfs came home they undid the lace
and she revived miraculously.
She was as full of life as soda pop.
Beware of your stepmother,
they said.
She will try once more.

Snow White, the dumb bunny,
opened the door
and she bit into a poison apple
and fell down for the final time.
When the dwarfs returned
they undid her bodice,
they looked for a comb,

but it did no good.
Though they washed her with wine
and rubbed her with butter
it was to no avail.
She lay as still as a gold piece.

The seven dwarfs could not bring themselves
to bury her in the black ground
so they made a glass coffin
and set it upon the seventh mountain
so that all who passed by
could peek in upon her beauty.
A prince came one June day
and would not budge.
He stayed so long his hair turned green
and still he would not leave.
The dwarfs took pity upon him
and gave him the glass Snow White—
its doll's eyes shut forever—
to keep in his far-off castle.
As the prince's men carried the coffin
they stumbled and dropped it
and the chunk of apple flew out
of her throat and she woke up miraculously.

And thus Snow White became the prince's bride.
The wicked queen was invited to the wedding feast
and when she arrived there were
red-hot iron shoes,
in the manner of red-hot roller skates,
clamped upon her feet.
First your toes will smoke
and then your heels will turn black
and you will fry upward like a frog,
she was told.
And so she danced until she was dead,
a subterranean figure,

her tongue flicking in and out
like a gas jet.
Meanwhile Snow White held court,
rolling her china-blue doll eyes open and shut
and sometimes referring to her mirror
as women do.

CINDERELLA

You always read about it:
the plumber with twelve children
who wins the Irish Sweepstakes.
From toilets to riches.
That story.

Or the nursemaid,
some luscious sweet from Denmark
who captures the oldest son's heart.
From diapers to Dior.
That story.

Or a milkman who serves the wealthy,
eggs, cream, butter, yogurt, milk,
the white truck like an ambulance
who goes into real estate
and makes a pile.
From homogenized to martinis at lunch.

Or the charwoman
who is on the bus when it cracks up
and collects enough from the insurance.
From mops to Bonwit Teller.
That story.

Once
the wife of a rich man was on her deathbed

and she said to her daughter Cinderella:
Be devout. Be good. Then I will smile
down from heaven in the seam of a cloud.
The man took another wife who had
two daughters, pretty enough
but with hearts like blackjacks.
Cinderella was their maid.
She slept on the sooty hearth each night
and walked around looking like Al Jolson.
Her father brought presents home from town,
jewels and gowns for the other women
but the twig of a tree for Cinderella.
She planted that twig on her mother's grave
and it grew to a tree where a white dove sat.
Whenever she wished for anything the dove
would drop it like an egg upon the ground.
The bird is important, my dears, so heed him.

Next came the ball, as you all know.
It was a marriage market.
The prince was looking for a wife.
All but Cinderella were preparing
and gussying up for the big event.
Cinderella begged to go too.
Her stepmother threw a dish of lentils
into the cinders and said: Pick them
up in an hour and you shall go.
The white dove brought all his friends;
all the warm wings of the fatherland came,
and picked up the lentils in a jiffy.
No, Cinderella, said the stepmother,
you have no clothes and cannot dance.
That's the way with stepmothers.

Cinderella went to the tree at the grave
and cried forth like a gospel singer:
Mama! Mama! My turtledove,

send me to the prince's ball!
The bird dropped down a golden dress
and delicate little gold slippers.
Rather a large package for a simple bird.
So she went. Which is no surprise.
Her stepmother and sisters didn't
recognize her without her cinder face
and the prince took her hand on the spot
and danced with no other the whole day.

As nightfall came she thought she'd better
get home. The prince walked her home
and she disappeared into the pigeon house
and although the prince took an axe and broke
it open she was gone. Back to her cinders.
These events repeated themselves for three days.
However on the third day the prince
covered the palace steps with cobbler's wax
and Cinderella's gold shoe stuck upon it.
Now he would find whom the shoe fit
and find his strange dancing girl for keeps.
He went to their house and the two sisters
were delighted because they had lovely feet.
The eldest went into a room to try the slipper on
but her big toe got in the way so she simply
sliced it off and put on the slipper.
The prince rode away with her until the white dove
told him to look at the blood pouring forth.
That is the way with amputations.
They don't just heal up like a wish.
The other sister cut off her heel
but the blood told as blood will.
The prince was getting tired.
He began to feel like a shoe salesman.
But he gave it one last try.
This time Cinderella fit into the shoe
like a love letter into its envelope.

At the wedding ceremony
the two sisters came to curry favor
and the white dove pecked their eyes out.
Two hollow spots were left
like soup spoons.

Cinderella and the prince
lived, they say, happily ever after,
like two dolls in a museum case
never bothered by diapers or dust,
never arguing over the timing of an egg,
never telling the same story twice,
never getting a middle-aged spread,
their darling smiles pasted on for eternity.
Regular Bobbsey Twins.
That story.

THE WITCH'S LIFE

When I was a child
there was an old woman in our neighborhood
whom we called The Witch.
All day she peered from her second story window
from behind the wrinkled curtains
and sometimes she would open the window
and yell: Get out of my life!
She had hair like kelp
and a voice like a boulder.

I think of her sometimes now
and wonder if I am becoming her.
My shoes turn up like a jester's.
Clumps of my hair, as I write this,
curl up individually like toes.
I am shoveling the children out,
scoop after scoop.

Only my books anoint me,
and a few friends,
those who reach into my veins.
Maybe I am becoming a hermit,
opening the door for only
a few special animals?
Maybe my skull is too crowded
and it has no opening through which
to feed it soup?
Maybe I have plugged up my sockets
to keep the gods in?
Maybe, although my heart
is a kitten of butter,
I am blowing it up like a zeppelin.
Yes. It is the witch's life,
climbing the primordial climb,
a dream within a dream,
then sitting here
holding a basket of fire.

THE PLAY

I am the only actor.
It is difficult for one woman
to act out a whole play.
The play is my life,
my solo act.
My running after the hands
and never catching up.
(The hands are out of sight—
that is, offstage.)
All I am doing onstage is running,
running to keep up,
but never making it.

Suddenly I stop running.
(This moves the plot along a bit.)

I give speeches, hundreds,
all prayers, all soliloquies.
I say absurd things like:
eggs must not quarrel with stones
or, keep your broken arm inside your sleeve
or, I am standing upright
but my shadow is crooked.
And such and such.
Many boos. Many boos.

Despite that I go on to the last lines:
To be without God is to be a snake
who wants to swallow an elephant.
The curtain falls.
The audience rushes out.
It was a bad performance.
That's because I'm the only actor
and there are few humans whose lives
will make an interesting play.
Don't you agree?

STAR-NOSED MOLE

Mole, angel-dog of the pit,
digging six miles a night,
what's up with you in your sooty suit,
where's your kitchen at?

I find you at the edge of our pond,
drowned, numb drainer of weeds,
insects floating in your belly,
grubs like little fetuses bobbing

and your dear face with its fifth hand,
doesn't it know it's the end of the war?
It's all over, no need to go deep into ponds,
no fires, no cripples left.

Mole dog,
I wish your mother would wake you up
and you wouldn't lie there like the Pietà
wearing your cross on your nose.

EARTHWORM

Slim inquirer, while the old fathers sleep
you are reworking their soil, you have
a grocery store there down under the earth
and it is well stocked with broken wine bottles,
old cigars, old door knobs and earth,
that great brown flour that you kiss each day.
There are dark stars in the cool evening and
you fondle them like killer birds' beaks.
But what I want to know is why when small boys
dig you up for curiosity and cut you in half
why each half lives and crawls away as if whole.
Have you no beginning and end? Which heart is
the real one? Which eye the seer? Why
is it in the infinite plan that you would
be severed and rise from the dead like a gargoyle
with two heads?

JANUARY 1ST

*Today is favorable for joint financial affairs but do not take any chances
with speculation.*

My daddy played the market.
My mother cut her coupons.
The children ran in circles.
The maid announced, the soup's on.

The guns were cleaned on Sunday.
The family went out to shoot.

We sat in the blind for hours.
The ducks fell down like fruit.

The big fat war was going on.
So profitable for daddy.
She drove a pea green Ford.
He drove a pearl gray Caddy.

In the end they used it up.
All that pale green dough.
The rest I spent on doctors
who took it like gigolos.

My financial affairs are small.
Indeed they seem to shrink.
My heart is on a budget.
It keeps me on the brink.

I tell it stories now and then
and feed it images like honey.
I will not speculate today
with poems that think they're money.

MARCH 4TH

Improve your finances.

The high ones, Berryman said, die, die, die.
You look up and who is there?
Daddy's not there shaking his money cane.
Mother's not there waving dollars good-bye
or coughing diamonds into her hanky. Not a forbear,
not an aunt or a chick to call me by name,
not the gardener with his candy dimes and tickles,
not grandpa with his bag full of nickels.

They are all embalmed with their cash
and there is no one here but us kids.
You and me lapping stamps and paying
the bills, shoveling up the beans and the hash.
Our checks are pale. Our wallets are invalids.
Past due, past due, is what our bills are saying
and yet we kiss in every corner, scuffing the dust
and the cat. Love rises like bread as we go bust.

SYLVIA PLATH

At the time of her death at the age of thirty, Sylvia Plath had published one somewhat derivative collection of poems, *The Colossus,* and, under a pseudonym, a sour autobiographical novel called *The Bell Jar.* If it is remarkable that she should be found in a selective anthology, it is equally remarkable that no one conversant with contemporary letters is likely to find her inclusion at all unusual. There is a poignant irony in the fact that this gifted woman, who hungered for recognition during her brief lifetime, was awarded a Pulitzer Prize nineteen years after she died, that the paperback edition of *The Bell Jar* has had sales in the hundreds of thousands, and that *Ariel,* published two years after her death, is among the best-selling volumes of poetry in English to appear in this century.

It is *Ariel* and two other posthumous works, *Crossing the Water* (mostly composed between *The Colossus* and *Ariel*) and *Winter Trees* (written during the *Ariel* period), that account for Plath's secure place in literary history. The domestic drama behind these last poems has fired the imagination not only of those devoted to compelling art but also of those fascinated by the often unruly lives of artists, to the point that biographies and memoirs about the poet have become something of a cottage industry.

Plath was living in Devon, England, with her husband, the charismatic Yorkshire poet Ted Hughes, and their two young children when she discovered that he was involved with another woman, the wife of a friend. She felt abandoned. Over a period of several months following this revelation, first in Devon and then in a London apartment, she composed in a kind of white heat the disturbing lyrics that revealed aspects of her inner life until then unexpressed. She was aware of the work's power and, referring to herself as a genius, wrote to her mother "I am writing the best poems of my life; they will make my name."

During one single month, October 1962, she finished twenty-five poems characterized by what Hughes called "crackling verbal energy," including "Lady Lazarus," spoken by a thirty-year-old woman who every decade attempts to kill herself: "Dying / is an art, like everything else. / I do it exceptionally well." Then one morning in February 1963, during the early hour when much of her most brilliant work had been written, after having sealed off the room where her children slept, the poet turned on the gas oven and took her life—and nearly that of a downstairs neighbor. The manuscript Plath left behind was reshaped by Hughes, her legal heir (he removed some "personally aggressive" work), and eventually *Ariel* appeared in both England and the United States. The rest is literary history of an especially dramatic sort.

The poet's sense of being abandoned by her powerful husband after their six intense years together apparently repeated feelings she experienced following the death of her autocratic father, Otto, a German immigrant who taught entomology at Boston University and whose primary interest was bumblebees. Sylvia was eight at the time, and she later said she was never happy again ("I adored and despised him"). Her nemesis in "Lady Lazarus" is called Herr Doktor, Herr Enemy, and Herr Lucifer; as Saul Malkoff has observed, this figure represents "psychiatrist, father, husband, death itself, all responded to with love and hate. . . . Persecuted by an unfeeling world . . . she becomes the archetypal victim." Although the "Daddy" figure appears in several works, Janet Malcolm, in a probing study of Plath biographies, suggests that it may have been not the loss of her father but rather an unhealthy relationship with her possessive mother that provides a key to the mystery of her troubled life.

After Otto Plath's death, his widow, Aurelia, moved with

Sylvia and her brother from Winthrop Center, a seaside town near Boston, to Wellesley. Sylvia (who had her first poem published at eight), already a controlled perfectionist, won a scholarship to Smith, where she earned high grades, was courted by young men who tended to fall in love with her, and had stories and poems accepted by *Seventeen* and other magazines. These outward successes, however, masked a strong fear of failure and recurring states of depression, and following a month-long guest editorship at *Mademoiselle* in New York, she ingested an overdose of pills, surviving only because her grandmother heard moaning from the secluded place where Sylvia had hidden herself. After five months in a sanitarium ("a time of darkness, despair, disillusion") and a course of electroshock therapy (crude by today's standards), she recovered sufficiently to complete her undergraduate education and to win a Fulbright scholarship to Cambridge University.

Her meeting Hughes in London ended her quest for a "colossus" who was an intellectual equal. They were married soon afterward, eventually settling in rural Devon, after first spending a year in the States, where Plath taught at the alma mater she had so recently left. It was during this period that, along with Anne Sexton, she audited Robert Lowell's poetry class. Lowell, who later wrote a somewhat bizarre introduction to *Ariel,* described her as "willowy, long-waisted, sharp-elbowed, nervous, giggly, gracious—a brilliant, tense presence, embarrassed by restraint." He never guessed, he wrote, "her later appalling and triumphant fulfillment."

Plath's technically impressive early work, in both fiction and verse, is more well-behaved than spontaneous, betraying explicit debts to such models as Lowell, Sexton, Hughes, and especially Roethke. Like a dutiful student conscious of a teacher's tastes, she tended to cut her poetic cloth to fit the aesthetic standards of certain editors. Not until later, when she began to write for herself and, in the process, to risk speaking the unspeakable, did she discover her true voice. Two brief excerpts, one from *The Colossus* and the second from *Ariel,* suggest something of her progress from work that is competent but not especially memorable to a personal language, concise, mysterious, and disturbingly subtle.

> Mother, mother, what illbred aunt
> Or what disfigured and unsightly
> Cousin did you so unwisely keep
> Unasked to my christening, that she
> Sent these ladies in her stead
> With heads like darning-eggs to nod
> And nod and nod at foot and head
> And at the left side of my crib?
> (from "The Disquieting Muses")

> The woman is perfected.
> Her dead

> Body wears the smile of accomplishment,
> The illusion of a Greek necessity

> Flows in the scrolls of her toga,
> Her bare

> Feet seem to be saying:
> We have come so far, it is over.
> (from "Edge")

The Pulitzer prize was awarded to *The Collected Poems,* edited by Hughes and published by Harper & Row in 1981; an attractive paperback appeared in 1992. This volume, which provides brief biographical comments for each year from 1956 to 1963 and explanatory notes for some of the poems, contains all the work from the four published books as well as other poems and a section of "juvenilia," fifty undistinguished lyrics composed before 1956. The volume offers a clear picture of the dramatic maturation of a brilliant artist.

I have selected just two lyrics ("Mushrooms" and "The Beekeeper's Daughter") from *The Colossus* and, not surprisingly, several from the work of the final months. What is a bit surprising (at least to me) is that in reading the *Collected Poems* over and over I find myself increasingly drawn to certain lyrics in *Crossing the Water,* work that preceded the poet's separation from her husband. These lyrics, while disturbing and original, are both more accessible and less overwrought than many of those from the *Ariel* period. They contain fewer private (and therefore obscure) references and less of the rhetorical overkill that has the poet's speaker likening herself, as she does in "Lady Lazarus," to a concentration-camp victim. The British critic John Carey is not alone in disliking the tendency of both Lowell and Plath to appropriate historical tragedies "as if they were upsets in their own little psyches."

I concur with those readers who especially value the incandescent work composed during Plath's blazing final weeks, but I would encourage anyone drawn to this poet to spend time with *The Collected Poems* and especially *Crossing the Water.* Even so modest a suggestion may cause my excommunication from the congregation of those who have translated Plath into a cult figure and martyr and portrayed Hughes, possibly unfairly, as a villain. I put it this way because nobody other than the two participants themselves can ever truly know what takes place, day by day, hour by hour, within a marriage. The moment has surely come for a moratorium on biographical speculation and, instead, for celebration of an extraordinary body of work.

The Collected Poems, edited by Ted Hughes (Harper & Row, 1981). For biography, see Janet Malcolm, *The Silent Woman: Sylvia Plath & Ted Hughes* (Alfred A. Knopf, 1994).

THE BEEKEEPER'S DAUGHTER

A garden of mouthings. Purple, scarlet-speckled, black
The great corollas dilate, peeling back their silks.
Their musk encroaches, circle after circle,

A well of scents almost too dense to breathe in.
Hieratical in your frock coat, maestro of the bees,
You move among the many-breasted hives,

My heart under your foot, sister of a stone.

Trumpet-throats open to the beaks of birds.
The Golden Rain Tree drips its powders down.
In these little boudoirs streaked with orange and red
The anthers nod their heads, potent as kings
To father dynasties. The air is rich.
Here is a queenship no mother can contest—

A fruit that's death to taste: dark flesh, dark parings.

In burrows narrow as a finger, solitary bees
Keep house among the grasses. Kneeling down
I set my eye to a hole-mouth and meet an eye
Round, green, disconsolate as a tear.
Father, bridegroom, in this Easter egg
Under the coronal of sugar roses

The queen bee marries the winter of your year.

MUSHROOMS

Overnight, very
Whitely, discreetly,
Very quietly

Our toes, our noses
Take hold on the loam,
Acquire the air.

Nobody sees us,
Stops us, betrays us;
The small grains make room.

Soft fists insist on
Heaving the needles,
The leafy bedding,

Even the paving.
Our hammers, our rams,
Earless and eyeless,

Perfectly voiceless,
Widen the crannies,
Shoulder through holes. We

Diet on water,
On crumbs of shadow,
Bland-mannered, asking

Little or nothing.
So many of us!
So many of us!

We are shelves, we are
Tables, we are meek,
We are edible,

Nudgers and shovers
In spite of ourselves.
Our kind multiplies:

We shall by morning
Inherit the earth.
Our foot's in the door.

YOU'RE

Clownlike, happiest on your hands,
Feet to the stars, and moon-skulled,

Gilled like a fish. A common-sense
Thumbs-down on the dodo's mode.
Wrapped up in yourself like a spool,
Trawling your dark as owls do.
Mute as a turnip from the Fourth
Of July to All Fools' Day,
O high-riser, my little loaf.

Vague as fog and looked for like mail.
Farther off than Australia.
Bent-backed Atlas, our traveled prawn.
Snug as a bud and at home
Like a sprat in a pickle jug.
A creel of eels, all ripples.
Jumpy as a Mexican bean.
Right, like a well-done sum.
A clean slate, with your own face on.

MORNING SONG

Love set you going like a fat gold watch.
The midwife slapped your footsoles, and your bald cry
Took its place among the elements.

Our voices echo, magnifying your arrival. New statue.
In a drafty museum, your nakedness
Shadows our safety. We stand round blankly as walls.

I'm no more your mother
Than the cloud that distills a mirror to reflect its own slow
Effacement at the wind's hand.

All night your moth-breath
Flickers among the flat pink roses. I wake to listen:
A far sea moves in my ear.

One cry, and I stumble from bed, cow-heavy and floral
In my Victorian nightgown.
Your mouth opens clean as a cat's. The window square

Whitens and swallows its dull stars. And now you try
Your handful of notes;
The clear vowels rise like balloons.

TULIPS

The tulips are too excitable, it is winter here.
Look how white everything is, how quiet, how snowed-in.
I am learning peacefulness, lying by myself quietly
As the light lies on these white walls, this bed, these hands.
I am nobody; I have nothing to do with explosions.
I have given my name and my day-clothes up to the nurses
And my history to the anesthetist and my body to surgeons.

They have propped my head between the pillow and the
    sheet-cuff
Like an eye between two white lids that will not shut.
Stupid pupil, it has to take everything in.
The nurses pass and pass, they are no trouble,
They pass the way gulls pass inland in their white caps,
Doing things with their hands, one just the same as another,
So it is impossible to tell how many there are.

My body is a pebble to them, they tend it as water
Tends to the pebbles it must run over, smoothing them
    gently.
They bring me numbness in their bright needles, they bring
    me sleep.
Now I have lost myself I am sick of baggage——
My patent leather overnight case like a black pillbox,
My husband and child smiling out of the family photo;
Their smiles catch onto my skin, little smiling hooks.

I have let things slip, a thirty-year-old cargo boat
Stubbornly hanging on to my name and address.
They have swabbed me clear of my loving associations.
Scared and bare on the green plastic-pillowed trolley
I watched my teaset, my bureaus of linen, my books
Sink out of sight, and the water went over my head.
I am a nun now, I have never been so pure.

I didn't want any flowers, I only wanted
To lie with my hands turned up and be utterly empty.
How free it is, you have no idea how free——
The peacefulness is so big it dazes you,
And it asks nothing, a name tag, a few trinkets.
It is what the dead close on, finally; I imagine them
Shutting their mouths on it, like a Communion tablet.

The tulips are too red in the first place, they hurt me.
Even through the gift paper I could hear them breathe
Lightly, through their white swaddlings, like an awful baby.
Their redness talks to my wound, it corresponds.
They are subtle: they seem to float, though they weigh me
    down,
Upsetting me with their sudden tongues and their color,
A dozen red lead sinkers round my neck.

Nobody watched me before, now I am watched.
The tulips turn to me, and the window behind me
Where once a day the light slowly widens and slowly thins,
And I see myself, flat, ridiculous, a cut-paper shadow
Between the eye of the sun and the eyes of the tulips,
And I have no face, I have wanted to efface myself.
The vivid tulips eat my oxygen.

Before they came the air was calm enough,
Coming and going, breath by breath, without any fuss.
Then the tulips filled it up like a loud noise.
Now the air snags and eddies round them the way a river

Snags and eddies round a sunken rust-red engine.
They concentrate my attention, that was happy
Playing and resting without committing itself.

The walls, also, seem to be warming themselves.
The tulips should be behind bars like dangerous animals;
They are opening like the mouth of some great African cat,
And I am aware of my heart: it opens and closes
Its bowl of red blooms out of sheer love of me.
The water I taste is warm and salt, like the sea,
And comes from a country far away as health.

INSOMNIAC

The night sky is only a sort of carbon paper,
Blueblack, with the much-poked periods of stars
Letting in the light, peephole after peephole—
A bonewhite light, like death, behind all things.
Under the eyes of the stars and the moon's rictus
He suffers his desert pillow, sleeplessness
Stretching its fine, irritating sand in all directions.

Over and over the old, granular movie
Exposes embarrassments—the mizzling days
Of childhood and adolescence, sticky with dreams,
Parental faces on tall stalks, alternately stern and tearful,
A garden of buggy roses that made him cry.
His forehead is bumpy as a sack of rocks.
Memories jostle each other for face-room like obsolete film
     stars.

He is immune to pills: red, purple, blue—
How they lit the tedium of the protracted evening!
Those sugary planets whose influence won for him
A life baptized in no-life for a while,
And the sweet, drugged waking of a forgetful baby.

Now the pills are worn-out and silly, like classical gods.
Their poppy-sleepy colors do him no good.

His head is a little interior of gray mirrors.
Each gesture flees immediately down an alley
Of diminishing perspectives, and its significance
Drains like water out the hole at the far end.
He lives without privacy in a lidless room,
The bald slots of his eyes stiffened wide-open
On the incessant heat-lightning flicker of situations.

Nightlong, in the granite yard, invisible cats
Have been howling like women, or damaged instruments.
Already he can feel daylight, his white disease,
Creeping up with her hatful of trivial repetitions.
The city is a map of cheerful twitters now,
And everywhere people, eyes mica-silver and blank,
Are riding to work in rows, as if recently brainwashed.

THE BABYSITTERS

It is ten years, now, since we rowed to Children's Island.
The sun flamed straight down that noon on the water off
    Marblehead.
That summer we wore black glasses to hide our eyes.
We were always crying, in our spare rooms, little put-upon
    sisters,
In the two huge, white, handsome houses in Swampscott.
When the sweetheart from England appeared, with her cream
    skin and Yardley cosmetics,
I had to sleep in the same room with the baby on a too-short
    cot,
And the seven-year-old wouldn't go out unless his jersey
    stripes
Matched the stripes of his socks.

O it was richness!—eleven rooms and a yacht
With a polished mahogany stair to let into the water
And a cabin boy who could decorate cakes in six-colored
    frosting.
But I didn't know how to cook, and babies depressed me.
Nights, I wrote in my diary spitefully, my fingers red
With triangular scorch marks from ironing tiny ruchings and
    puffed sleeves.
When the sporty wife and her doctor husband went on one
    of their cruises
They left me a borrowed maid named Ellen, 'for protection',
And a small Dalmatian.

In your house, the main house, you were better off.
You had a rose garden and a guest cottage and a model
    apothecary shop
And a cook and a maid, and knew about the key to the
    bourbon.
I remember you playing 'Ja Da' in a pink piqué dress
On the gameroom piano, when the 'big people' were out,
And the maid smoked and shot pool under a green-shaded
    lamp.
The cook had one wall eye and couldn't sleep, she was so
    nervous.
On trial, from Ireland, she burned batch after batch of
    cookies
Till she was fired.

O what has come over us, my sister!
On that day-off the two of us cried so hard to get
We lifted a sugared ham and a pineapple from the grownups'
    icebox
And rented an old green boat. I rowed. You read
Aloud, crosslegged on the stern seat, from the *Generation of
    Vipers*.
So we bobbed out to the island. It was deserted—
A gallery of creaking porches and still interiors,

Stopped and awful as a photograph of somebody laughing,
But ten years dead.

The bold gulls dove as if they owned it all.
We picked up sticks of driftwood and beat them off,
Then stepped down the steep beach shelf and into the water.
We kicked and talked. The thick salt kept us up.
I see us floating there yet, inseparable—two cork dolls.
What keyhole have we slipped through, what door has shut?
The shadows of the grasses inched round like hands of a
    clock,
And from our opposite continents we wave and call.
Everything has happened.

CROSSING THE WATER

Black lake, black boat, two black, cut-paper people.
Where do the black trees go that drink here?
Their shadows must cover Canada.

A little light is filtering from the water flowers.
Their leaves do not wish us to hurry:
They are round and flat and full of dark advice.

Cold worlds shake from the oar.
The spirit of blackness is in us, it is in the fishes.
A snag is lifting a valedictory, pale hand;

Stars open among the lilies.
Are you not blinded by such expressionless sirens?
This is the silence of astounded souls.

PHEASANT

You said you would kill it this morning.
Do not kill it. It startles me still,
The jut of that odd, dark head, pacing

Through the uncut grass on the elm's hill.
It is something to own a pheasant,
Or just to be visited at all.

I am not mystical: it isn't
As if I thought it had a spirit.
It is simply in its element.

That gives it a kingliness, a right.
The print of its big foot last winter,
The tail-track, on the snow in our court—

The wonder of it, in that pallor,
Through crosshatch of sparrow and starling.
Is it its rareness, then? It is rare.

But a dozen would be worth having,
A hundred, on that hill—green and red,
Crossing and recrossing: a fine thing!

It is such a good shape, so vivid.
It's a little cornucopia.
It unclaps, brown as a leaf, and loud,

Settles in the elm, and is easy.
It was sunning in the narcissi.
I trespass stupidly. Let be, let be.

For a Fatherless Son

You will be aware of an absence, presently,
Growing beside you, like a tree,
A death tree, color gone, an Australian gum tree—
Balding, gelded by lightning—an illusion,
And a sky like a pig's backside, an utter lack of attention.

But right now you are dumb.
And I love your stupidity,
The blind mirror of it. I look in
And find no face but my own, and you think that's funny.
It is good for me

To have you grab my nose, a ladder rung.
One day you may touch what's wrong
The small skulls, the smashed blue hills, the godawful hush.
Till then your smiles are found money.

The Arrival of the Bee Box

I ordered this, this clean wood box
Square as a chair and almost too heavy to lift.
I would say it was the coffin of a midget
Or a square baby
Were there not such a din in it.

The box is locked, it is dangerous.
I have to live with it overnight
And I can't keep away from it.
There are no windows, so I can't see what is in there.
There is only a little grid, no exit.

I put my eye to the grid.
It is dark, dark,

With the swarmy feeling of African hands
Minute and shrunk for export,
Black on black, angrily clambering.

How can I let them out?
It is the noise that appalls me most of all,
The unintelligible syllables.
It is like a Roman mob,
Small, taken one by one, but my god, together!

I lay my ear to furious Latin.
I am not a Caesar.
I have simply ordered a box of maniacs.
They can be sent back.
They can die, I need feed them nothing, I am the owner.

I wonder how hungry they are.
I wonder if they would forget me
If I just undid the locks and stood back and turned into a
    tree.
There is the laburnum, its blond colonnades,
And the petticoats of the cherry.

They might ignore me immediately
In my moon suit and funeral veil.
I am no source of honey
So why should they turn on me?
Tomorrow I will be sweet God, I will set them free.

The box is only temporary.

The Applicant

First, are you our sort of a person?
Do you wear
A glass eye, false teeth or a crutch,

A brace or a hook,
Rubber breasts or a rubber crotch,

Stitches to show something's missing? No, no? Then
How can we give you a thing?
Stop crying.
Open your hand.
Empty? Empty. Here is a hand

To fill it and willing
To bring teacups and roll away headaches
And do whatever you tell it.
Will you marry it?
It is guaranteed

To thumb shut your eyes at the end
And dissolve of sorrow.
We make new stock from the salt.
I notice you are stark naked.
How about this suit——

Black and stiff, but not a bad fit.
Will you marry it?
It is waterproof, shatterproof, proof
Against fire and bombs through the roof.
Believe me, they'll bury you in it.

Now your head, excuse me, is empty.
I have the ticket for that.
Come here, sweetie, out of the closet.
Well, what do you think of *that*?
Naked as paper to start

But in twenty-five years she'll be silver,
In fifty, gold.
A living doll, everywhere you look.
It can sew, it can cook,
It can talk, talk, talk.

It works, there is nothing wrong with it.
You have a hole, it's a poultice.
You have an eye, it's an image.
My boy, it's your last resort.
Will you marry it, marry it, marry it.

Daddy

You do not do, you do not do
Any more, black shoe
In which I have lived like a foot
For thirty years, poor and white,
Barely daring to breathe or Achoo.

Daddy, I have had to kill you.
You died before I had time——
Marble-heavy, a bag full of God,
Ghastly statue with one gray toe
Big as a Frisco seal

And a head in the freakish Atlantic
Where it pours bean green over blue
In the waters off beautiful Nauset.
I used to pray to recover you.
Ach, du.

In the German tongue, in the Polish town
Scraped flat by the roller
Of wars, wars, wars.
But the name of the town is common.
My Polack friend

Says there are a dozen or two.
So I never could tell where you
Put your foot, your root,
I never could talk to you.
The tongue stuck in my jaw.

It stuck in a barb wire snare.
Ich, ich, ich, ich,
I could hardly speak.
I thought every German was you.
And the language obscene

An engine, an engine
Chuffing me off like a Jew.
A Jew to Dachau, Auschwitz, Belsen.
I began to talk like a Jew.
I think I may well be a Jew.

The snows of the Tyrol, the clear beer of Vienna
Are not very pure or true.
With my gipsy ancestress and my weird luck
And my Taroc pack and my Taroc pack
I may be a bit of a Jew.

I have always been scared of *you,*
With your Luftwaffe, your gobbledygoo.
And your neat mustache
And your Aryan eye, bright blue.
Panzer-man, panzer-man, O You——

Not God but a swastika
So black no sky could squeak through.
Every woman adores a Fascist,
The boot in the face, the brute
Brute heart of a brute like you.

You stand at the blackboard, daddy,
In the picture I have of you,
A cleft in your chin instead of your foot
But no less a devil for that, no not
Any less the black man who

Bit my pretty red heart in two.
I was ten when they buried you.

At twenty I tried to die
And get back, back, back to you.
I thought even the bones would do.

But they pulled me out of the sack,
And they stuck me together with glue.
And then I knew what to do.
I made a model of you,
A man in black with a Meinkampf look

And a love of the rack and the screw.
And I said I do, I do.
So daddy, I'm finally through.
The black telephone's off at the root,
The voices just can't worm through.

If I've killed one man, I've killed two——
The vampire who said he was you
And drank my blood for a year,
Seven years, if you want to know.
Daddy, you can lie back now.

There's a stake in your fat black heart
And the villagers never liked you.
They are dancing and stamping on you.
They always *knew* it was you.
Daddy, daddy, you bastard, I'm through.

LADY LAZARUS

I have done it again.
One year in every ten
I manage it——

A sort of walking miracle, my skin
Bright as a Nazi lampshade,
My right foot

A paperweight,
My face a featureless, fine
Jew linen.

Peel off the napkin
O my enemy.
Do I terrify?——

The nose, the eye pits, the full set of teeth?
The sour breath
Will vanish in a day.

Soon, soon the flesh
The grave cave ate will be
At home on me

And I a smiling woman.
I am only thirty.
And like the cat I have nine times to die.

This is Number Three.
What a trash
To annihilate each decade.

What a million filaments.
The peanut-crunching crowd
Shoves in to see

Them unwrap me hand and foot——
The big strip tease.
Gentlemen, ladies

These are my hands
My knees.
I may be skin and bone,

Nevertheless, I am the same, identical woman.
The first time it happened I was ten.
It was an accident.

The second time I meant
To last it out and not come back at all.
I rocked shut

As a seashell.
They had to call and call
And pick the worms off me like sticky pearls.

Dying
Is an art, like everything else.
I do it exceptionally well.

I do it so it feels like hell.
I do it so it feels real.
I guess you could say I've a call.

It's easy enough to do it in a cell.
It's easy enough to do it and stay put.
It's the theatrical

Comeback in broad day
To the same place, the same face, the same brute
Amused shout:

'A miracle!'
That knocks me out.
There is a charge

For the eyeing of my scars, there is a charge
For the hearing of my heart——
It really goes.

And there is a charge, a very large charge
For a word or a touch
Or a bit of blood

Or a piece of my hair or my clothes.
So, so, Herr Doktor.
So, Herr Enemy.

I am your opus,
I am your valuable,
The pure gold baby

That melts to a shriek.
I turn and burn.
Do not think I underestimate your great concern.

Ash, ash—
You poke and stir.
Flesh, bone, there is nothing there——

A cake of soap,
A wedding ring,
A gold filling.

Herr God, Herr Lucifer
Beware
Beware.

Out of the ash
I rise with my red hair
And I eat men like air.

CHILD

Your clear eye is the one absolutely beautiful thing.
I want to fill it with color and ducks,
The zoo of the new

Whose names you meditate—
April snowdrop, Indian pipe,
Little

Stalk without wrinkle,
Pool in which images
Should be grand and classical

Not this troublous
Wringing of hands, this dark
Ceiling without a star.

BALLOONS

Since Christmas they have lived with us,
Guileless and clear,
Oval soul-animals,
Taking up half the space,
Moving and rubbing on the silk

Invisible air drifts,
Giving a shriek and pop
When attacked, then scooting to rest, barely trembling.
Yellow cathead, blue fish——
Such queer moons we live with

Instead of dead furniture!
Straw mats, white walls
And these traveling
Globes of thin air, red, green,
Delighting

The heart like wishes or free
Peacocks blessing
Old ground with a feather
Beaten in starry metals.
Your small

Brother is making
His balloon squeak like a cat.
Seeming to see
A funny pink world he might eat on the other side of it,
He bites,

Then sits
Back, fat jug
Contemplating a world clear as water.
A red
Shred in his little fist.

ALLEN GINSBERG

Allen Ginsberg is represented in *The Harvard Book of Contemporary American Poetry,* published in 1985, by more pages than are allotted any other contributor. This implicit conferring of a literary gold medal by editor Helen Vendler doubtless raises the eyebrows (and hackles) of those who persist in thinking of Ginsberg as a hirsute beatnik notable largely for using four-letter words, celebrating homosexual love, and experimenting with mind-altering drugs. The editor's recognition, though, was not only understandable but even overdue. Ginsberg, who regarded all his works as fragments in a great confession, may well be the most uneven major poet who ever put pen to paper—the distance between his strongest work and his weakest is immense—but at his best he clearly stands in the front rank of American artists.

Everything about Ginsberg invites a kind of hyperbole. The best-known poet of our time, he is also the best loved and most reviled. And he is one of the most prolific: his *Collected Poems, 1947–1980,* handsomely produced by Harper & Row in 1984, runs more than 800 pages, and yet according to his biographer, Michael Schumacher, it contains less than one percent of his work. Schumacher's *Dharma Lion* (Ginsberg's Buddhist name) itself weighs in at just under 800 pages and, at that, takes the poet only to 1981, with a postscript summarizing the details of the 1980s.

Ginsberg's celebrated public readings also had a larger-than-life quality: chanting mantras, playing finger cymbals, and reciting his poems—occasionally composed on the spot—he attracted the sorts of immense crowds (sometimes in the tens of thousands) generally associated with rock stars. It is no exaggeration to say that for many years he was to serious poetry what the Beatles (or Bob Dylan) were to popular music. In the words of John Ashbery, "I think he's changed the role of the poet in America. Now everybody experiences poetry. It's much closer to us . . . and I think that is due not only to his poetry but to his truly exemplary way of living."

Irwin Allen Ginsberg was born June 3, 1926, in Newark, New Jersey. His father, Louis, a high school English teacher and poet, acquired a respectable reputation for his conventional lyrics. His mother, Naomi, an outspoken Communist born in the Soviet Union, suffered from severe paranoia that kept her in and out of mental hospitals during her son's formative years. At Columbia University (which expelled but later readmitted him) his closest friends included William Burroughs, author of *Naked Lunch,* and Jack Kerouac, whose theory of spontaneous composition, exemplified in *On the Road* and other novels, influenced Ginsberg. It was Kerouac who first used the word *beat* (as in "beatific" and "beatitude") to characterize an approach to literature with which Ginsberg has been regularly identified. The young poet also developed an intense emotional relationship with the charismatic Neal Cassady, the model for Kerouac's most memorable fictional creation.

Ginsberg had other important literary models as well. He was profoundly moved by William Blake's mystical vision and by Whitman's incantatory rhythms, uninhibited self-revelation, and celebration of the brotherhood of man. Like Whitman he demonstrated, in Peter Conn's apt phrase, the apocalyptic zest of a minor prophet. His most powerful influence was another New Jerseyan, William Carlos Williams, who rejected British literary models in favor of the idiomatic language of Americans. "Before I met Williams," Ginsberg said, "I was all hung up on cats like Wyatt, Surrey, and Donne. . . . He told me 'Listen to the rhythm of your own voice. Proceed intuitively by ear.' " Williams was a father figure to a generation of aspiring poets in much the way that Ginsberg, generous in his support of others, was himself to become a model and guru to countless young writers.

The poet's early writing efforts attracted some attention, but it was the publication in 1956 of *Howl,* with its highly charged opening lines, that made him a household name.

I saw the best minds of my generation destroyed by madness,
    starving hysterical naked,
dragging themselves through the negro streets at dawn
    looking for an angry fix,
angelheaded hipsters burning for the ancient heavenly
    connection to the starry dynamo in the machinery of
    night,
who poverty and tatters and hollow-eyed and high sat up
    smoking in the supernatural darkness of cold-water flats
    floating across the tops of cities contemplating jazz,
who bared their brains to Heaven under the El and saw
    Mohammedan angels staggering on tenement roofs
    illuminated,
who passed through universities with radiant cool eyes
    hallucinating Arkansas and Blake-light tragedy among the
    scholars of war,
who were expelled from the academies for crazy &
    publishing
    obscene odes on the windows of the skull,
who cowered in unshaven rooms in underwear, burning their
    money in wastebaskets and listening to the Terror through
    the wall,
who got busted in their pubic beards returning through
    Laredo
    with a belt of marijuana for New York,
who ate fire in paint hotels or drank turpentine in Paradise
    Alley, death, or purgatoried their torsos night after
    night
with dreams, with drugs, with waking nightmares . . .

This poem (the subject of a 1957 obscenity trial in San Francisco), much of it written in one sitting, is dedicated to Carl Solomon, a highly intelligent man Ginsberg got to know during eight months he was required to spend in the Columbia University Psychiatric Institute during his early twenties, having pled insanity to avoid imprisonment after being wrongly implicated in a friend's illegal activities. Ginsberg was aware that in *Howl* he had created a "new poetry," work that in the words of Michael Schumacher "brought together the influences of Whitman and Williams, the American idiom, elements of jazz, the philosophy of the Beat Generation, the spontaneous writing style of Jack Kerouac, Ginsberg's homage to Cézanne, his sympathy for Carl Solomon and other friends, and autobiographical detail." In a perceptive review of the poem, M. L. Rosenthal refers to Ginsberg's as a poetry of genuine suffering: "He has brought a terrible psychological reality to the surface with enough originality to blast American verse a hair's breadth forward in the process."

The poet's most celebrated work, *Kaddish* (1961), is a moving elegy for his mother, based loosely on the Hebrew lament for the dead. This harrowing work was made into a play in 1972. The poet also tried his hand at an opera, *Hydrogen Jukebox,* with music by Philip Glass, performed at the Spoleto Festival in 1990. In addition he has composed thousands of pages of a personal journal, much of the liveliest material describing his travels. During his most active years he gave readings not only throughout the United States but all over the world. Invariably he spoke without inhibitions about his long-term relationship with the poet Peter Orlovsky and about his liberal views, even in such repressive places as Cuba, Czechoslovakia, Poland (he once played a lute on a Warsaw street corner, attired in a loincloth), China, and the Soviet Union; on more than one occasion he was invited (to put it gently) to leave on the next available flight. He marched in the anti–Vietnam War "flower-power" protests in the 1960s, was arrested (along with Benjamin Spock) during an antidraft protest, and participated in the demonstrations at the 1968 Democratic convention in Chicago. He was also twice arrested for protesting the use and spread of nuclear energy.

In his sixties Ginsberg took a serious interest in photography; exhibitions of his work have been held in Los Angeles, Chicago, and elsewhere. He continued to teach at Brooklyn College and the Naropa School of Disembodied Poetics in Colorado, to support the work of young artists, and to oppose censorship of any sort—*Howl* has been the focus of controversies regarding "indecency" over the radio airwaves. An active member of PEN, the international association of writers, he was especially effective in championing the cause of individual freedom.

I once sat next to him during a tedious PEN board meeting and watched as he filled a page with symbolic pictorial images influenced by his Buddhist philosophy. When I expressed admiration for the handsome design, he unhesitatingly gave it to me—it is hanging above my desk as I write. Such spontaneous generosity would not surprise anyone who knew this sociable man. Allen Ginsberg died of cancer in 1997 at age 70, but his spirit clearly survives in the lives of those drawn to his robust work and generous presence.

Collected Poems, 1947–1980 (Harper & Row, 1984); *Cosmopolitan Greetings: Poems 1986–1992* (HarperCollins, 1994). Michael Schumacher, *Dharma Lion: A Critical Biography of Allen Ginsberg* (St. Martin's Press, 1992).

A Supermarket in California

What thoughts I have of you tonight, Walt Whitman, for I walked down the sidestreets under the trees with a headache self-conscious looking at the full moon.

In my hungry fatigue, and shopping for images, I went into the neon fruit supermarket, dreaming of your enumerations!

What peaches and what penumbras! Whole families shopping at night! Aisles full of husbands! Wives in the avocados, babies in the tomatoes!—and you, García Lorca, what were you doing down by the watermelons?

I saw you, Walt Whitman, childless, lonely old grubber, poking among the meats in the refrigerator and eyeing the grocery boys.

I heard you asking questions of each: Who killed the pork chops? What price bananas? Are you my Angel?

I wandered in and out of the brilliant stacks of cans following you, and followed in my imagination by the store detective.

We strode down the open corridors together in our solitary fancy tasting artichokes, possessing every frozen delicacy, and never passing the cashier.

Where are we going, Walt Whitman? The doors close in an hour. Which way does your beard point tonight?

(I touch your book and dream of our odyssey in the supermarket and feel absurd.)

Will we walk all night through solitary streets? The trees add shade to shade, lights out in the houses, we'll both be lonely.

Will we stroll dreaming of the lost America of love past blue automobiles in driveways, home to our silent cottage?

Ah, dear father, graybeard, lonely old courage-teacher, what America did you have when Charon quit poling his ferry and you got out on a smoking bank and stood watching the boat disappear on the black waters of Lethe?

SUNFLOWER SUTRA

I walked on the banks of the tincan banana dock and sat down
    under the huge shade of a Southern Pacific locomotive to
    look at the sunset over the box house hills and cry.
Jack Kerouac sat beside me on a busted rusty iron pole, compan-
    ion, we thought the same thoughts of the soul, bleak and blue
    and sad-eyed, surrounded by the gnarled steel roots of trees of
    machinery.

The oily water on the river mirrored the red sky, sun sank on
   top of final Frisco peaks, no fish in that stream, no hermit in
   those mounts, just ourselves rheumy-eyed and hung-over like
   old bums on the river-bank, tired and wily.
Look at the Sunflower, he said, there was a dead gray shadow
   against the sky, big as a man, sitting dry on top of a pile of
   ancient sawdust—
—I rushed up enchanted—it was my first sunflower, memories
   of Blake—my visions—Harlem
and Hells of the Eastern rivers, bridges clanking Joes Greasy
   Sandwiches, dead baby carriages, black treadless tires forgot-
   ten and unretreaded, the poem of the riverbank, condoms &
   pots, steel knives, nothing stainless, only the dank muck and
   the razor-sharp artifacts passing into the past—
and the gray Sunflower poised against the sunset, crackly bleak
   and dusty with the smut and smog and smoke of olden
   locomotives in its eye—
corolla of bleary spikes pushed down and broken like a battered
   crown, seeds fallen out of its face, soon-to-be-toothless
   mouth of sunny air, sunrays obliterated on its hairy head like
   a dried wire spiderweb,
leaves stuck out like arms out of the stem, gestures from the
   sawdust root, broke pieces of plaster fallen out of the black
   twigs, a dead fly in its ear,
Unholy battered old thing you were, my sunflower O my soul,
   I loved you then!
The grime was no man's grime but death and human locomo-
   tives,
all that dress of dust, that veil of darkened railroad skin, that smog
   of cheek, that eyelid of black mis'ry, that sooty hand or phallus
   or protuberance of artificial worse-than-dirt—industrial—
   modern—all that civilization spotting your crazy golden
   crown—
and those blear thoughts of death and dusty loveless eyes and
   ends and withered roots below, in the home-pile of sand and
   sawdust, rubber dollar bills, skin of machinery, the guts and
   innards of the weeping coughing car, the empty lonely tincans

with their rusty tongues alack, what more could I name, the
smoked ashes of some cock cigar, the cunts of wheelbarrows
and the milky breasts of cars, wornout asses out of chairs &
sphincters of dynamos—all these
entangled in your mummied roots—and you there standing
before me in the sunset, all your glory in your form!
A perfect beauty of a sunflower! a perfect excellent lovely sun-
flower existence! a sweet natural eye to the new hip moon,
woke up alive and excited grasping in the sunset shadow
sunrise golden monthly breeze!
How many flies buzzed round you innocent of your grime,
while you cursed the heavens of the railroad and your flower
soul?
Poor dead flower? when did you forget you were a flower?
when did you look at your skin and decide you were an
impotent dirty old locomotive? the ghost of a locomotive? the
specter and shade of a once powerful mad American locomo-
tive?
You were never no locomotive, Sunflower, you were a sun-
flower!
And you Locomotive, you are a locomotive, forget me not!
So I grabbed up the skeleton thick sunflower and stuck it at my
side like a scepter,
and deliver my sermon to my soul, and Jack's soul too, and
anyone who'll listen,
—We're not our skin of grime, we're not our dread bleak dusty
imageless locomotive, we're all golden sunflowers inside,
blessed by our own seed & hairy naked accomplishment-
bodies growing into mad black formal sunflowers in the sun-
set, spied on by our eyes under the shadow of the mad
locomotive riverbank sunset Frisco hilly tincan evening sit-
down vision.

AMERICA

America I've given you all and now I'm nothing.
America two dollars and twentyseven cents January 17, 1956.
I can't stand my own mind.
America when will we end the human war?
Go fuck yourself with your atom bomb.
I don't feel good don't bother me.
I won't write my poem till I'm in my right mind.
America when will you be angelic?
When will you take off your clothes?
When will you look at yourself through the grave?
When will you be worthy of your million Trotskyites?
America why are your libraries full of tears?
America when will you send your eggs to India?
I'm sick of your insane demands.
When can I go into the supermarket and buy what I need with
    my good looks?
America after all it is you and I who are perfect not the next
    world.
Your machinery is too much for me.
You made me want to be a saint.
There must be some other way to settle this argument.
Burroughs is in Tangiers I don't think he'll come back it's
    sinister.
Are you being sinister or is this some form of practical joke?
I'm trying to come to the point.
I refuse to give up my obsession.
America stop pushing I know what I'm doing.
America the plum blossoms are falling.
I haven't read the newspapers for months, everyday somebody
    goes on trial for murder.
America I feel sentimental about the Wobblies.
America I used to be a communist when I was a kid I'm not
    sorry.
I smoke marijuana every chance I get.

I sit in my house for days on end and stare at the roses in the closet.

When I go to Chinatown I get drunk and never get laid.

My mind is made up there's going to be trouble.

You should have seen me reading Marx.

My psychoanalyst thinks I'm perfectly right.

I won't say the Lord's Prayer.

I have mystical visions and cosmic vibrations.

America I still haven't told you what you did to Uncle Max after he came over from Russia.

I'm addressing you.

Are you going to let your emotional life be run by Time Magazine?

I'm obsessed by Time Magazine.

I read it every week.

Its cover stares at me every time I slink past the corner candystore.

I read it in the basement of the Berkeley Public Library.

It's always telling me about responsibility. Businessmen are serious. Movie producers are serious. Everybody's serious but me.

It occurs to me that I am America.

I am talking to myself again.

Asia is rising against me.

I haven't got a chinaman's chance.

I'd better consider my national resources.

My national resources consist of two joints of marijuana millions of genitals an unpublishable private literature that jetplanes 1400 miles an hour and twentyfive-thousand mental institutions.

I say nothing about my prisons nor the millions of underprivileged who live in my flowerpots under the light of five hundred suns.

I have abolished the whorehouses of France, Tangiers is the next to go.

My ambition is to be President despite the fact that I'm a Catholic.

America how can I write a holy litany in your silly mood?
I will continue like Henry Ford my strophes are as individual as his automobiles more so they're all different sexes.
America I will sell you strophes $2500 apiece $500 down on your old strophe
America free Tom Mooney
America save the Spanish Loyalists
America Sacco & Vanzetti must not die
America I am the Scottsboro boys.
America when I was seven momma took me to Communist Cell meetings they sold us garbanzos a handful per ticket a ticket costs a nickel and the speeches were free everybody was angelic and sentimental about the workers it was all so sincere you have no idea what a good thing the party was in 1835 Scott Nearing was a grand old man a real mensch Mother Bloor the Silk-strikers' Ewig-Weibliche made me cry I once saw the Yiddish orator Israel Amter plain. Everybody must have been a spy.
America you don't really want to go to war.
America it's them bad Russians.
Them Russians them Russians and them Chinamen. And them Russians.
The Russia wants to eat us alive. The Russia's power mad. She wants to take our cars from out our garages.
Her wants to grab Chicago. Her needs a Red *Reader's Digest*. Her wants our auto plants in Siberia. Him big bureaucracy running our fillingstations.
That no good. Ugh. Him make Indians learn read. Him need big black niggers. Hah. Her make us all work sixteen hours a day. Help.
America this is quite serious.
America this is the impression I get from looking in the television set.

America is this correct?
I'd better get right down to the job.
It's true I don't want to join the Army or turn lathes in precision
    parts factories, I'm nearsighted and psychopathic anyway.
America I'm putting my queer shoulder to the wheel.

THE LION FOR REAL

"Soyez muette pour moi, Idole contemplative . . . "

I came home and found a lion in my living room
Rushed out on the fire escape screaming Lion! Lion!
Two stenographers pulled their brunette hair and banged the
    window shut
I hurried home to Paterson and stayed two days.

Called up my old Reichian analyst
who'd kicked me out of therapy for smoking marijuana
'It's happened' I panted 'There's a Lion in my room'
'I'm afraid any discussion would have no value' he hung up.

I went to my old boyfriend we got drunk with his girlfriend
I kissed him and announced I had a lion with a mad gleam in my
    eye
We wound up fighting on the floor I bit his eyebrow & he
    kicked me out
I ended masturbating in his jeep parked in the street moaning
    'Lion.'

Found Joey my novelist friend and roared at him 'Lion!'
He looked at me interested and read me his spontaneous ignu
    high poetries
I listened for lions all I heard was Elephant Tiglon Hippogriff
    Unicorn Ants
But figured he really understood me when we made it in Ignaz
    Wisdom's bathroom.

But next day he sent me a leaf from his Smoky Mountain retreat
'I love you little Bo-Bo with your delicate golden lions
But there being no Self and No Bars therefore the Zoo of your
    dear Father hath no Lion
You said your mother was mad don't expect me to produce the
    Monster for your Bridegroom.'

Confused dazed and exalted bethought me of real lion starved in
    his stink in Harlem
Opened the door the room was filled with the bomb blast of his
    anger
He roaring hungrily at the plaster walls but nobody could hear
    him outside thru the window
My eye caught the edge of the red neighbor apartment building
    standing in deafening stillness

We gazed at each other his implacable yellow eye in the red halo
    of fur
Waxed rheumy on my own but he stopped roaring and bared a
    fang greeting.
I turned my back and cooked broccoli for supper on an iron gas
    stove
boilt water and took a hot bath in the old tub under the sink
    board.

He didn't eat me, tho I regretted him starving in my presence.
Next week he wasted away a sick rug full of bones wheaten hair
    falling out
enraged and reddening eye as he lay aching huge hairy head on
    his paws
by the egg-crate bookcase filled up with thin volumes of Plato,
    & Buddha.

Sat by his side every night averting my eyes from his hungry
    motheaten face
stopped eating myself he got weaker and roared at night while
    I had nightmares

Eaten by lion in bookstore on Cosmic Campus, a lion myself
    starved by Professor Kandisky, dying in a lion's flophouse
    circus,
I woke up mornings the lion still added dying on the floor—
    'Terrible Presence!' I cried 'Eat me or die!'

It got up that afternoon—walked to the door with its paw on the
    wall to steady its trembling body
Let out a soul-rending creak from the bottomless roof of his
    mouth
thundering from my floor to heaven heavier than a volcano at
    night in Mexico
Pushed the door open and said in a gravelly voice "Not this time
    Baby—but I will be back again."

Lion that eats my mind now for a decade knowing only your
    hunger
Not the bliss of your satisfaction O roar of the Universe how am
    I chosen
In this life I have heard your promise I am ready to die I have
    served
Your starved and ancient Presence O Lord I wait in my room
    at your Mercy.

MY SAD SELF

TO FRANK O'HARA

Sometimes when my eyes are red
I go up on top of the RCA Building
        and gaze at my world, Manhattan—
            my buildings, streets I've done feats in,
                lofts, beds, coldwater flats
        —on Fifth Ave below which I also bear in mind,
            its ant cars, little yellow taxis, men
                walking the size of specks of wool—

Panorama of the bridges, sunrise over Brooklyn machine,
       sun go down over New Jersey where I was born
          & Paterson where I played with ants—
my later loves on 15th Street,
       my greater loves of Lower East Side,
          my once fabulous amours in the Bronx
                    faraway—
paths crossing in these hidden streets,
    my history summed up, my absences
       and ecstasies in Harlem—
    —sun shining down on all I own
       in one eyeblink to the horizon
          in my last eternity—
                         matter is water.

Sad,
    I take the elevator and go
          down, pondering,
and walk on the pavements staring into all man's
                         plateglass, faces,
          questioning after who loves,
    and stop, bemused
       in front of an automobile shopwindow
    standing lost in calm thought,
       traffic moving up & down 5th Avenue blocks behind me
          waiting for a moment when . . .

Time to go home & cook supper & listen to
          the romantic war news on the radio
                    . . . all movement stops
& I walk in the timeless sadness of existence,
       tenderness flowing thru the buildings,
          my fingertips touching reality's face,
       my own face streaked with tears in the mirror
          of some window—at dusk—
                         where I have no desire—

for bonbons—or to own the dresses or Japanese
        lampshades of intellection—

Confused by the spectacle around me,
      Man struggling up the street
          with packages, newspapers,
                      ties, beautiful suits
          toward his desire
      Man, woman, streaming over the pavements
          red lights clocking hurried watches &
            movements at the curb—

And all these streets leading
      so crosswise, honking, lengthily,
          by avenues
     stalked by high buildings or crusted into slums
          thru such halting traffic
               screaming cars and engines
so painfully to this
      countryside, this graveyard
        this stillness
               on deathbed or mountain
    once seen
          never regained or desired
            in the mind to come
where all Manhattan that I've seen must disappear.

KADDISH

FOR NAOMI GINSBERG, 1894–1956

I

Strange now to think of you, gone without corsets & eyes, while
   I walk on the sunny pavement of Greenwich Village.
downtown Manhattan, clear winter noon, and I've been up all
   night, talking, talking, reading the Kaddish aloud, listening to
   Ray Charles blues shout blind on the phonograph

the rhythm the rhythm—and your memory in my head three
   years after—And read Adonais' last triumphant stanzas
   aloud—wept, realizing how we suffer—
And how Death is that remedy all singers dream of, sing, re-
   member, prophesy as in the Hebrew Anthem, or the Buddhist
   Book of Answers—and my own imagination of a withered
   leaf—at dawn—
Dreaming back thru life, Your time—and mine accelerating
   toward Apocalypse,
the final moment—the flower burning in the Day—and what
   comes after,
looking back on the mind itself that saw an American city
a flash away, and the great dream of Me or China, or you and
   a phantom Russia, or a crumpled bed that never existed—
like a poem in the dark—escaped back to Oblivion—
No more to say, and nothing to weep for but the Beings in the
   Dream, trapped in its disappearance,
sighing, screaming with it, buying and selling pieces of phantom,
   worshipping each other,
worshipping the God included in it all—longing or inevitabil-
   ity?—while it lasts, a Vision—anything more?
It leaps about me, as I go out and walk the street, look back over
   my shoulder, Seventh Avenue, the battlements of window
   office buildings shouldering each other high, under a cloud,
   tall as the sky an instant—and the sky above—an old blue
   place.
or down the Avenue to the south, to—as I walk toward the
   Lower East Side—where you walked 50 years ago, little girl—
   from Russia, eating the first poisonous tomatoes of Amer-
   ica—frightened on the dock—
then struggling in the crowds of Orchard Street toward what?—
   toward Newark—
toward candy store, first home-made sodas of the century, hand-
   churned ice cream in backroom on musty brownfloor
   boards—
Toward education marriage nervous breakdown, operation,

teaching school, and learning to be mad, in a dream—what is this life?

Toward the Key in the window—and the great Key lays its head of light on top of Manhattan, and over the floor, and lays down on the sidewalk—in a single vast beam, moving, as I walk down First toward the Yiddish Theater—and the place of poverty

you knew, and I know, but without caring now—Strange to have moved thru Paterson, and the West, and Europe and here again,

with the cries of Spaniards now in the doorstoops doors and dark boys on the street, fire escapes old as you

—Tho you're not old now, that's left here with me—

Myself, anyhow, maybe as old as the universe—and I guess that dies with us—enough to cancel all that comes—What came is gone forever every time—

That's good! That leaves it open for no regret—no fear radiators, lacklove, torture even toothache in the end—

Though while it comes it is a lion that eats the soul—and the lamb, the soul, in us, alas, offering itself in sacrifice to change's fierce hunger—hair and teeth—and the roar of bonepain, skull bare, break rib, rot-skin, braintricked Implacability.

Ai! ai! we do worse! We are in a fix! And you're out, Death let you out, Death had the Mercy, you're done with your century, done with God, done with the path thru it—Done with yourself at last—Pure—Back to the Babe dark before your Father, before us all—before the world—

There, rest. No more suffering for you. I know where you've gone, it's good.

No more flowers in the summer fields of New York, no joy now, no more fear of Louis,

and no more of his sweetness and glasses, his high school decades, debts, loves, frightened telephone calls, conception beds, relatives, hands—

No more of sister Elanor,—she gone before you—we kept it secret—you killed her—or she killed herself to bear with you—an arthritic heart—But Death's killed you both—No matter—

Nor your memory of your mother, 1915 tears in silent movies weeks and weeks—forgetting, agrieve watching Marie Dressler address humanity, Chaplin dance in youth,

or Boris Godunov, Chaliapin's at the Met, halling his voice of a weeping Czar—by standing room with Elanor & Max—watching also the Capitalists take seats in Orchestra, white furs, diamonds,

with the YPSL's hitch-hiking thru Pennsylvania, in black baggy gym skirts pants, photograph of 4 girls holding each other round the waste, and laughing eye, too coy, virginal solitude of 1920

all girls grown old, or dead, now, and that long hair in the grave—lucky to have husbands later—

You made it—I came too—Eugene my brother before (still grieving now and will gream on to his last stiff hand, as he goes thru his cancer—or kill—later perhaps—soon he will think—)

And it's the last moment I remember, which I see them all, thru myself, now—tho not you

I didn't foresee what you felt—what more hideous gape of bad mouth came first—to you—and were you prepared?

To go where? In that Dark—that—in that God? a radiance? A Lord in the Void? Like an eye in the black cloud in a dream? Adonoi at last, with you?

Beyond my remembrance! Incapable to guess! Not merely the yellow skull in the grave, or a box of worm dust, and a stained ribbon—Deathshead with Halo? can you believe it?

Is it only the sun that shines once for the mind, only the flash of existence, than none ever was?

Nothing beyond what we have—what you had—that so pitiful—yet Triumph,

to have been here, and changed, like a tree, broken, or flower—fed to the ground—but mad, with its petals, colored, thinking Great Universe, shaken, cut in the head, leaf strip, hid in an egg crate hospital, cloth wrapped, sore—freaked in the moon brain, Naughtless.

No flower like that flower, which knew itself in the garden, and fought the knife—lost

Cut down by an idiot Snowman's icy—even in the Spring— strange ghost thought—some Death—Sharp icicle in his hand—crowned with old roses—a dog for his eyes—cock of a sweatshop—heart of electric irons.

All the accumulations of life, that wear us out—clocks, bodies, consciousness, shoes, breasts—begotten sons—your Communism—'Paranoia' into hospitals.

You once kicked Elanor in the leg, she died of heart failure later. You of stroke. Asleep? within a year, the two of you, sisters in death. Is Elanor happy?

Max grieves alive in an office on Lower Broadway, lone large mustache over midnight Accountings, not sure. His life passes—as he sees—and what does he doubt now? Still dream of making money, or that might have made money, hired nurse, had children, found even your Immortality, Naomi?

I'll see him soon. Now I've got to cut through—to talk to you—as I didn't when you had a mouth.

Forever. And we're bound for that, Forever—like Emily Dickinson's horses—headed to the End.

They know the way—These Steeds—run faster than we think— it's our own life they cross—and take with them.

Magnificent, mourned no more, marred of heart, mind
behind, married dreamed, mortal changed—Ass and face
done with murder.

In the world, given, flower maddened, made no Utopia, shut
under pine, almed in Earth, balmed in Lone, Jehovah, accept.

Nameless, One Faced, Forever beyond me, beginningless,
endless, Father in death. Tho I am not there for this Prophecy,
I am unmarried, I'm hymnless, I'm Heavenless, headless in bliss-
hood I would still adore

Thee, Heaven, after Death, only One blessed in Nothingness,
not light or darkness, Dayless Eternity—

Take this, this Psalm, from me, burst from my hand in a day, some of my Time, now given to Nothing—to praise Thee—But Death

This is the end, the redemption from Wilderness, way for the Wonderer, House sought for All, black handkerchief washed clean by weeping—page beyond Psalm—Last change of mine and Naomi—to God's perfect Darkness—Death, stay thy phantoms!

II

Over and over—refrain—of the Hospitals—still haven't written your history—leave it abstract—a few images

run thru the mind—like the saxophone chorus of houses and years—remembrance of electrical shocks.

By long nites as a child in Paterson apartment, watching over your nervousness—you were fat—your next move—

By that afternoon I stayed home from school to take care of you—once and for all—when I vowed forever that once man disagreed with my opinion of the cosmos, I was lost—

By my later burden—vow to illuminate mankind—this is release of particulars—(mad as you)—(sanity a trick of agreement)—

But you stared out the window on the Broadway Church corner, and spied a mystical assassin from Newark,

So phoned the Doctor—'OK go way for a rest'—so I put on my coat and walked you downstreet—On the way a grammarschool boy screamed, unaccountably—'Where you goin Lady to Death'? I shuddered—

and you covered your nose with motheaten fur collar, gas mask against poison sneaked into downtown atmosphere, sprayed by Grandma—

And was the driver of the cheesebox Public Service bus a member of the gang? You shuddered at his face, I could hardly get you on—to New York, very Times Square, to grab another Greyhound—

where we hung around 2 hours fighting invisible bugs and jewish sickness—breeze poisoned by Roosevelt—

out to get you—and me tagging along, hoping it would end in a quiet room in a Victorian house by a lake.

Ride 3 hours thru tunnels past all American industry, Bayonne preparing for World War II, tanks, gas fields, soda factories, diners, locomotive roundhouse fortress—into piney woods New Jersey Indians—calm towns—long roads thru sandy tree fields—

Bridges by deerless creeks, old wampum loading the streambed—down there a tomahawk or Pocahontas bone—and a million old ladies voting for Roosevelt in brown small houses, roads off the Madness highway—

perhaps a hawk in a tree, or a hermit looking for an owl-filled branch—

All the time arguing—afraid of strangers in the forward double seat, snoring regardless—what busride they snore on now?

'Allen, you don't understand—it's—ever since those 3 big sticks up my back—they did something to me in Hospital, they poisoned me, they want to see me dead—3 big sticks, 3 big sticks—

'The Bitch! Old Grandma! Last week I saw her, dressed in pants like an old man, with a sack on her back, climbing up the brick side of the apartment

'On the fire escape, with poison germs, to throw on me—at night—maybe Louis is helping her—he's under her power—

'I'm your mother, take me to Lakewood' (near where Graf Zeppelin had crashed before, all Hitler in Explosion) 'where I can hide.'

We got there—Dr. Whatzis rest home—she hid behind a closet—demanded a blood transfusion.

We were kicked out—tramping with Valise to unknown shady lawn houses—dusk, pine trees after dark—long dead street filled with crickets and poison ivy—

I shut her up by now—big house REST HOME ROOMS—gave the landlady her money for the week—carried up the iron valise—sat on bed waiting to escape—

Neat room in attic with friendly bedcover—lace curtains—

spinning wheel rug—Stained wallpaper old as Naomi. We were home.

I left on the next bus to New York—laid my head back in the last seat, depressed—the worst yet to come?—abandoning her, rode in torpor—I was only 12.

Would she hide in her room and come out cheerful for breakfast? Or lock her door and stare thru the window for sidestreet spies? Listen at keyholes for Hitlerian invisible gas? Dream in a chair—or mock me, by—in front of a mirror, alone?

12 riding the bus at nite thru New Jersey, have left Naomi to Parcae in Lakewood's haunted house—left to my own fate bus—sunk in a seat—all violins broken—my heart sore in my ribs—mind was empty—Would she were safe in her coffin—

Or back at Normal School in Newark, studying up on America in a black skirt—winter on the street without lunch—a penny a pickle—home at night to take care of Elanor in the bedroom—

First nervous breakdown was 1919—she stayed home from school and lay in a dark room for three weeks—something bad—never said what—every noise hurt—dreams of the creaks of Wall Street—

Before the gray Depression—went upstate New York—recovered—Lou took photo of her sitting crossleg on the grass—her long hair wound with flowers—smiling—playing lullabies on mandolin—poison ivy smoke in left-wing summer camps and me in infancy saw trees—

or back teaching school, laughing with idiots, the backward classes—her Russian specialty—morons with dreamy lips, great eyes, thin feet & sicky fingers, swaybacked, rachitic—

great heads pendulous over Alice in Wonderland, a blackboard full of C A T.

Naomi reading patiently, story out of a Communist fairy book—Tale of the Sudden Sweetness of the Dictator—Forgiveness of Warlocks—Armies Kissing—

Deathsheads Around the Green Table—The King & the

Workers—Paterson Press printed them up in the '30s till she went mad, or they folded, both.

O Paterson! I got home late that nite. Louis was worried. How could I be so—didn't I think? I shouldn't have left her. Mad in Lakewood. Call the Doctor. Phone the home in the pines. Too late.

Went to bed exhausted, wanting to leave the world (probably that year newly in love with R——my high school mind hero, jewish boy who came a doctor later—then silent neat kid—

I later laying down life for him, moved to Manhattan— followed him to college—Prayed on ferry to help mankind if admitted—vowed, the day I journeyed to Entrance Exam—

by being honest revolutionary labor lawyer—would train for that—inspired by Sacco Vanzetti, Norman Thomas, Debs, Altgeld, Sandburg, Poe—Little Blue Books. I wanted to be President, or Senator.

ignorant woe—later dreams of kneeling by R's shocked knees declaring my love of 1941—What sweetness he'd have shown me, tho, that I'd wished him & despaired—first love—a crush—

Later a mortal avalanche, whole mountains of homosexuality, Matterhorns of cock, Grand Canyons of asshole—weight on my melancholy head—

meanwhile I walked on Broadway imagining Infinity like a rubber ball without space beyond—what's outside?—coming home to Graham Avenue still melancholy passing the lone green hedges across the street, dreaming after the movies—)

The telephone rang at 2 A.M.—Emergency—she'd gone mad—Naomi hiding under the bed screaming bugs of Mussolini—Help! Louis! Buba! Fascists! Death!—the landlady frightened—old fag attendant screaming back at her—

Terror, that woke the neighbors—old ladies on the second floor recovering from menopause—all those rags between thighs, clean sheets, sorry over lost babies—husbands ashen— children sneering at Yale, or putting oil in hair at CCNY—or trembling in Montclair State Teachers College like Eugene—

Her big leg crouched to her breast, hand outstretched Keep Away, wool dress on her thighs, fur coat dragged under the bed—she barricaded herself under bedspring with suitcases.

Louis in pajamas listening to phone, frightened—do now?—Who could know?—my fault, delivering her to solitude?—sitting in the dark room on the sofa, trembling, to figure out—

He took the morning train to Lakewood, Naomi still under bed—thought he brought poison Cops—Naomi screaming—Louis what happened to your heart then? Have you been killed by Naomi's ecstasy?

Dragged her out, around the corner, a cab, forced her in with valise, but the driver left them off at drugstore. Bus stop, two hours' wait.

I lay in bed nervous in the 4-room apartment, the big bed in living room, next to Louis' desk—shaking—he came home that nite, late, told me what happened.

Naomi at the prescription counter defending herself from the enemy—racks of children's books, douche bags, aspirins, pots, blood—'Don't come near me—murderers! Keep away! Promise not to kill me!'

Louis in horror at the soda fountain—with Lakewood girl-scouts—Coke addicts—nurses—busmen hung on schedule—Police from country precinct, dumbed—and a priest dreaming of pigs on an ancient cliff?

Smelling the air—Louis pointing to emptiness?—Customers vomiting their Cokes—or staring—Louis humiliated—Naomi triumphant—The Announcement of the Plot. Bus arrives, the drivers won't have them on trip to New York.

Phonecalls to Dr. Whatzis, 'She needs a rest,' The mental hospital—State Greystone Doctors—'Bring her here, Mr. Ginsberg.'

Naomi, Naomi—sweating, bulge-eyed, fat, the dress unbuttoned at one side—hair over brow, her stocking hanging evilly on her legs—screaming for a blood transfusion—one righteous hand upraised—a shoe in it—barefoot in the Pharmacy—

The enemies approach—what poisons? Tape recorders? FBI?

Zhdanov hiding behind the counter? Trotsky mixing rat bacteria in the back of the store? Uncle Sam in Newark, plotting deathly perfumes in the Negro district? Uncle Ephraim, drunk with murder in the politician's bar, scheming of Hague? Aunt Rose passing water thru the needles of the Spanish Civil War?

till the hired $35 ambulance came from Red Bank—— Grabbed her arms—strapped her on the stretcher—moaning, poisoned by imaginaries, vomiting chemicals thru Jersey, begging mercy from Essex County to Morristown—

And back to Greystone where she lay three years—that was the last breakthrough, delivered her to Madhouse again—

On what wards—I walked there later, oft—old catatonic ladies, gray as cloud or ash or walls—sit crooning over floorspace—Chairs—and the wrinkled hags acreep, accusing— begging my 13-year-old mercy—

'Take me home'—I went alone sometimes looking for the lost Naomi, taking Shock—and I'd say, 'No, you're crazy Mama,—Trust the Drs.'—

And Eugene, my brother, her elder son, away studying Law in a furnished room in Newark—

came Paterson-ward next day—and he sat on the brokendown couch in the living room—'We had to send her back to Greystone'—

—his face perplexed, so young, then eyes with tears—then crept weeping all over his face—'What for?' wail vibrating in his cheekbones, eyes closed up, high voice—Eugene's face of pain.

Him faraway, escaped to an Elevator in the Newark Library, his bottle daily milk on windowsill of $5 week furn room downtown at trolley tracks—

He worked 8 hrs. a day for $20/wk—thru Law School years— stayed by himself innocent near negro whorehouses.

Unlaid, poor virgin—writing poems about Ideals and politics letters to the editor Pat Eve News—(we both wrote, denouncing Senator Borah and Isolationists—and felt mysterious toward Paterson City Hall—

I sneaked inside it once—local Moloch tower with phallus

spire & cap o' ornament, strange gothic Poetry that stood on
Market Street—replica Lyons' Hotel de Ville—

wings, balcony & scrollwork portals, gateway to the giant city
clock, secret map room full of Hawthorne—dark Debs in the
Board of Tax—Rembrandt smoking in the gloom—

Silent polished desks in the great committee room—Alder-
men? Bd of Finance? Mosca the hairdresser aplot—Crapp the
gangster issuing orders from the john—The madmen struggling
over Zone, Fire, Cops & Backroom Metaphysics—we're all
dead—outside by the bus stop Eugene stared thru childhood—

where the Evangelist preached madly for 3 decades, hard-
haired, cracked & true to his mean Bible—chalked Prepare to
Meet Thy God on civic pave—

or God is Love on the railroad overpass concrete—he raved
like I would rave, the lone Evangelist—Death on City Hall—)

But Gene, young,—been Montclair Teachers College 4
years—taught half year & quit to go ahead in life—afraid of
Discipline Problems—dark sex Italian students, raw girls getting
laid, no English, sonnets disregarded—and he did not know
much—just that he lost—

so broke his life in two and paid for Law—read huge blue
books and rode the ancient elevator 13 miles away in Newark
& studied up hard for the future

just found the Scream of Naomi on his failure doorstep, for
the final time, Naomi gone, us lonely—home—him sitting
there—

Then have some chicken soup, Eugene. The Man of Evangel
wails in front of City Hall. And this year Lou has poetic loves of
suburb middle age—in secret—music from his 1937 book—
Sincere—he longs for beauty—

No love since Naomi screamed—since 1923?—now lost in
Greystone ward—new shock for her—Electricity, following the
40 Insulin.

And Metrazol had made her fat.

So that a few years later she came home again—we'd much
advanced and planned—I waited for that day—my Mother again

to cook &—play the piano—sing at mandolin—Lung Stew, &
Stenka Razin, & the communist line on the war with Finland—
and Louis in debt—suspected to be poisoned money—mysteri-
ous capitalisms

—& walked down the long front hall & looked at the furni-
ture. She never remembered it all. Some amnesia. Examined the
doilies—and the dining room set was sold—

the Mahogany table—20 years love—gone to the junk man—
we still had the piano—and the book of Poe—and the Mando-
lin, tho needed some string, dusty—

She went to the backroom to lie down in bed and ruminate,
or nap, hide—I went in with her, not leave her by herself—lay
in bed next to her—shades pulled, dusky, late afternoon—Louis
in front room at desk, waiting—perhaps boiling chicken for
supper—

'Don't be afraid of me because I'm just coming back home
from the mental hospital—I'm your mother—'

Poor love, lost—a fear—I lay there—Said, 'I love you
Naomi,'—stiff, next to her arm. I would have cried, was this the
comfortless lone union?—Nervous, and she got up soon.

Was she ever satisfied? And—by herself sat on the new couch
by the front windows, uneasy—cheek leaning on her hand—
narrowing eye—at what fate that day—

Picking her tooth with her nail, lips formed an O, suspicion—
thought's old worn vagina—absent sideglance of eye—some evil
debt written in the wall, unpaid—& the aged breasts of Newark
come near—

May have heard radio gossip thru the wires in her head,
controlled by 3 big sticks left in her back by gangsters in amnesia,
thru the hospital—caused pain between her shoulders—

Into her head—Roosevelt should know her case, she told
me—Afraid to kill her, now, that the government knew their
names—traced back to Hitler—wanted to leave Louis' house
forever.

One night, sudden attack—her noise in the bathroom—like
croaking up her soul—convulsions and red vomit coming out of

her mouth—diarrhea water exploding from her behind—on all fours in front of the toilet—urine running between her legs— left retching on the tile floor smeared with her black feces— unfainted—

At forty, varicosed, nude, fat, doomed, hiding outside the apartment door near the elevator calling Police, yelling for her girlfriend Rose to help—

Once locked herself in with razor or iodine—could hear her cough in tears at sink—Lou broke through glass green-painted door, we pulled her out to the bedroom.

Then quiet for months that winter—walks, alone, nearby on Broadway, read Daily Worker—Broke her arm, fell on icy street—

Began to scheme escape from cosmic financial murder plots— later she ran away to the Bronx to her sister Elanor. And there's another saga of late Naomi in New York.

Or thru Elanor or the Workmen's Circle, where she worked, addressing envelopes, she made out—went shopping for Campbell's tomato soup—saved money Louis mailed her—

Later she found a boyfriend, and he was a doctor—Dr. Isaac worked for National Maritime Union—now Italian bald and pudgy old doll—who was himself an orphan—but they kicked him out—Old cruelties—

Sloppier, sat around on bed or chair, in corset dreaming to herself—'I'm hot—I'm getting fat—I used to have such a beautiful figure before I went to the hospital—You should have seen me in Woodbine—' This in a furnished room around the NMU hall, 1943.

Looking at naked baby pictures in the magazine—baby powder advertisements, strained lamb carrots—'I will think nothing but beautiful thoughts.'

Revolving her head round and round on her neck at window light in summertime, in hypnotize, in doven-dream recall—

'I touch his cheek, I touch his cheek, he touches my lips with his hand, I think beautiful thoughts, the baby has a beautiful hand.'—

Or a No-shake of her body, disgust—some thought of Buchenwald—some insulin passes thru her head—a grimace nerve shudder at Involuntary (as shudder when I piss)—bad chemical in her cortex—'No don't think of that. He's a rat.'

Naomi: 'And when we die we become an onion, a cabbage, a carrot, or a squash, a vegetable.' I come downtown from Columbia and agree. She reads the Bible, thinks beautiful thoughts all day.

'Yesterday I saw God. What did he look like? Well, in the afternoon I climbed up a ladder—he has a cheap cabin in the country, like Monroe, N.Y. the chicken farms in the wood. He was a lonely old man with a white beard.

'I cooked supper for him. I made him a nice supper—lentil soup, vegetables, bread & butter—miltz—he sat down at the table and ate, he was sad.

'I told him, Look at all those fightings and killings down there, What's the matter? Why don't you put a stop to it?

'I try, he said—That's all he could do, he looked tired. He's a bachelor so long, and he likes lentil soup.'

Serving me meanwhile, a plate of cold fish—chopped raw cabbage dript with tapwater—smelly tomatoes—week-old health food—grated beets & carrots with leaky juice, warm—more and more disconsolate food—I can't eat it for nausea sometimes—the Charity of her hands stinking with Manhattan, madness, desire to please me, cold undercooked fish—pale red near the bones. Her smells—and oft naked in the room, so that I stare ahead, or turn a book ignoring her.

One time I thought she was trying to make me come lay her—flirting to herself at sink—lay back on huge bed that filled most of the room, dress up round her hips, big slash of hair, scars of operations, pancreas, belly wounds, abortions, appendix, stitching of incisions pulling down in the fat like hideous thick zippers—ragged long lips between her legs—What, even, smell of asshole? I was cold—later revolted a little, not much—seemed perhaps a good idea to try—know the Monster of the Beginning Womb—Perhaps—that way. Would she care? She needs a lover.

Yisborach, v'yistabach, v'yispoar, v'yisroman, v'yisnaseh, v'yishador, v'yishalleh, v'yishallol, sh'meh d'kudsho, b'rich hu.

And Louis reestablishing himself in Paterson grimy apartment in negro district—living in dark rooms—but found himself a girl he later married, falling in love again—tho sere & shy—hurt with 20 years Naomi's mad idealism.

Once I came home, after longtime in N.Y., he's lonely— sitting in the bedroom, he at desk chair turned round to face me—weeps, tears in red eyes under his glasses—

That we'd left him—Gene gone strangely into army—she out on her own in N.Y., almost childish in her furnished room. So Louis walked downtown to postoffice to get mail, taught in highschool—stayed at poetry desk, forlorn—ate grief at Bickford's all these years—are gone.

Eugene got out of the Army, came home changed and lone— cut off his nose in jewish operation—for years stopped girls on Broadway for cups of coffee to get laid—Went to NYU, serious there, to finish Law.—

And Gene lived with her, ate naked fishcakes, cheap, while she got crazier—He got thin, or felt helpless, Naomi striking 1920 poses at the moon, half-naked in the next bed.

bit his nails and studied—was the weird nurse-son—Next year he moved to a room near Columbia—though she wanted to live with her children—

'Listen to your mother's plea, I beg you'—Louis still sending her checks—I was in bughouse that year 8 months—my own visions unmentioned in this here Lament—

But then went half mad—Hitler in her room, she saw his mustache in the sink—afraid of Dr. Isaac now, suspecting that he was in on the Newark plot—went up to Bronx to live near Elanor's Rheumatic Heart—

And Uncle Max never got up before noon, tho Naomi at 6 A.M. was listening to the radio for spies—or searching the windowsill,

for in the empty lot downstairs, an old man creeps with his bag stuffing packages of garbage in his hanging black overcoat.

Max's sister Edie works—17 years bookkeeper at Gimbels—

lived downstairs in apartment house, divorced—so Edie took in Naomi on Rochambeau Ave—

Woodlawn Cemetery across the street, vast dale of graves where Poe once—Last stop on Bronx subway—lots of communists in that area.

Who enrolled for painting classes at night in Bronx Adult High School—walked alone under Van Cortlandt Elevated line to class—paints Naomiisms—

Humans sitting on the grass in some Camp No-Worry summers yore—saints with droopy faces and long-ill-fitting pants, from hospital—

Brides in front of Lower East Side with short grooms—lost El trains running over the Babylonian apartment rooftops in the Bronx—

Sad paintings—but she expressed herself. Her mandolin gone, all strings broke in her head, she tried. Toward Beauty? or some old life Message?

But started kicking Elanor, and Elanor had heart trouble—came upstairs and asked her about Spydom for hours,—Elanor frazzled. Max away at office, accounting for cigar stores till at night.

'I am a great woman—am truly a beautiful soul—and because of that they (Hitler, Grandma, Hearst, the Capitalists, Franco, Daily News, the '20s, Mussolini, the living dead) want to shut me up—Buba's the head of a spider network—'

Kicking the girls, Edie & Elanor—Woke Edie at midnite to tell her she was a spy and Elanor a rat. Edie worked all day and couldn't take it—She was organizing the union.—And Elanor began dying, upstairs in bed.

The relatives call me up, she's getting worse—I was the only one left—Went on the subway with Eugene to see her, ate stale fish—

'My sister whispers in the radio—Louis must be in the apartment—his mother tells him what to say—LIARS!—I cooked for my two children—I played the mandolin—'

Last night the nightingale woke me / Last night when all was

still / it sang in the golden moonlight / from on the wintry hill.
She did.

I pushed her against the door and shouted 'DON'T KICK
ELANOR!'—she stared at me—Contempt—die—disbelief her
sons are so naive, so dumb—'Elanor is the worst spy! She's
taking orders!'

'—No wires in the room!'—I'm yelling at her—last ditch,
Eugene listening on the bed—what can he do to escape that fatal
Mama—'You've been away from Louis years already—
Grandma's too old to walk—'

We're all alive at once then—even me & Gene & Naomi in
one mythological Cousinesque room—screaming at each other
in the Forever—I in Columbia jacket, she half undressed.

I banging against her head which saw Radios, Sticks, Hit-
lers—the gamut of Hallucinations—for real—her own uni-
verse—no road that goes elsewhere—to my own—No America,
not even a world—

That you go as all men, as Van Gogh, as mad Hannah, all the
same—to the last doom—Thunder, Spirits, Lightning!

I've seen your grave! O strange Naomi! My own—cracked
grave! Shema Y'Israel—I am Svul Avrum—you—in death?

Your last night in the darkness of the Bronx—I phone-
called—thru hospital to secret police

that came, when you and I were alone, shrieking at Elanor in
my ear—who breathed hard in her own bed, got thin—

Nor will forget, the doorknock, at your fright of spies,—Law
advancing, on my honor—Eternity entering the room—you
running to the bathroom undressed, hiding in protest from the
last heroic fate—

staring at my eyes, betrayed—the final cops of madness rescu-
ing me—from your foot against the broken heart of Elanor,

your voice at Edie weary of Gimbels coming home to broken
radio—and Louis needing a poor divorce, he wants to get mar-
ried soon—Eugene dreaming, hiding at 125 St., suing negroes
for money on crud furniture, defending black girls—

Protests from the bathroom—Said you were sane—dressing in a cotton robe, your shoes, then new, your purse and newspaper clippings—no—your honesty—

as you vainly made your lips more real with lipstick, looking in the mirror to see if the Insanity was Me or a carful of police.

or Grandma spying at 78—Your vision—Her climbing over the walls of the cemetery with political kidnapper's bag—or what you saw on the walls of the Bronx, in pink nightgown at midnight, staring out the window on the empty lot—

Ah Rochambeau Ave.—Playground of Phantoms—last apartment in the Bronx for spies—last home for Elanor or Naomi, here these communist sisters lost their revolution—

'All right—put on your coat Mrs.—let's go—We have the wagon downstairs—you want to come with her to the station?'

The ride then—held Naomi's hand, and held her head to my breast, I'm taller—kissed her and said I did it for the best—Elanor sick—and Max with heart condition—Needs—

To me—'Why did you do this?'—'Yes Mrs., your son will have to leave you in an hour'—The Ambulance

came in a few hours—drove off at 4 A.M. to some Bellevue in the night downtown—gone to the hospital forever. I saw her led away—she waved, tears in her eyes.

Two years, after a trip to Mexico—bleak in the flat plain near Brentwood, scrub brush and grass around the unused RR train track to the crazyhouse—

new brick 20 story central building—lost on the vast lawns of madtown on Long Island—huge cities of the moon.

Asylum spreads out giant wings above the path to a minute black hole—the door—entrance thru crotch—

I went in—smelt funny—the halls again—up elevator—to a glass door on a Women's Ward—to Naomi—Two nurses buxom white—They led her out, Naomi stared—and I gaspt—She'd had a stroke—

Too thin, shrunk on her bones—age come to Naomi—now broken into white hair—loose dress on her skeleton—face sunk, old! withered—cheek of crone—

One hand stiff—heaviness of forties & menopause reduced by one heart stroke, lame now—wrinkles—a scar on her head, the lobotomy—ruin, the hand dipping downwards to death—

O Russian faced, woman on the grass, your long black hair is crowned with flowers, the mandolin is on your knees—

Communist beauty, sit here married in the summer among daisies, promised happiness at hand—

holy mother, now you smile on your love, your world is born anew, children run naked in the field spotted with dandelions,

they eat in the plum tree grove at the end of the meadow and find a cabin where a white-haired negro teaches the mystery of his rainbarrel—

blessed daughter come to America, I long to hear your voice again, remembering your mother's music, in the Song of the Natural Front—

O glorious muse that bore me from the womb, gave suck first mystic life & taught me talk and music, from whose pained head I first took Vision—

Tortured and beaten in the skull—What mad hallucinations of the damned that drive me out of my own skull to seek Eternity till I find Peace for Thee, O Poetry—and for all human-kind call on the Origin

Death which is the mother of the universe!—Now wear your nakedness forever, white flowers in your hair, your marriage sealed behind the sky—no revolution might destroy that mai-denhood—

O beautiful Garbo of my Karma—all photographs from 1920 in Camp Nicht-Gedeiget here unchanged—with all the teachers from Newark—Nor Elanor be gone, nor Max await his specter—nor Louis retire from this High School—

Back! You! Naomi! Skull on you! Gaunt immortality and revolution come—small broken woman—the ashen indoor eyes of hospitals, ward grayness on skin—

'Are you a spy?' I sat at the sour table, eyes filling with tears—'Who are you? Did Louis send you?—The wires—'

in her hair, as she beat on her head—'I'm not a bad girl—
don't murder me!—I hear the ceiling—I raised two children—'

Two years since I'd been there—I started to cry—She
stared—nurse broke up the meeting a moment—I went into the
bathroom to hide, against the toilet white walls

'The Horror' I weeping—to see her again—'The Horror'—
as if she were dead thru funeral rot in—'The Horror!'

I came back she yelled more—they led her away—'You're
not Allen—' I watched her face—but she passed by me, not
looking—

Opened the door to the ward,—she went thru without a
glance back, quiet suddenly—I stared out—she looked old—the
verge of the grave—'All the Horror!'

Another year, I left N.Y.—on West Coast in Berkeley cottage
dreamed of her soul—that, thru life, in what form it stood in that
body, ashen or manic, gone beyond joy—

near its death—with eyes—was my own love in its form, the
Naomi, my mother on earth still—sent her long letter—& wrote
hymns to the mad—Work of the merciful Lord of Poetry.

that causes the broken grass to be green, or the rock to break
in grass—or the Sun to be constant to earth—Sun of all sunflow-
ers and days on bright iron bridges—what shines on old hospi-
tals—as on my yard—

Returning from San Francisco one night, Orlovsky in my
room—Whalen in his peaceful chair—a telegram from Gene,
Naomi dead—

Outside I bent my head to the ground under the bushes near
the garage—knew she was better—

at last—not left to look on Earth alone—2 years of solitude—
no one, at age nearing 60—old woman of skulls—once long-
tressed Naomi of Bible—

or Ruth who wept in America—Rebecca aged in Newark—
David remembering his Harp, now lawyer at Yale

or Svul Avrum—Israel Abraham—myself—to sing in the wil-
derness toward God—O Elohim!—so to the end—2 days after
her death I got her letter—

Strange Prophecies anew! She wrote—'The key is in the window, the key is in the sunlight at the window—I have the key—Get married Allen don't take drugs—the key is in the bars, in the sunlight in the window.

Love,

your mother'

which is Naomi—

HYMMNN

In the world which He has created according to his will Blessed
  Praised

Magnified Lauded Exalted the Name of the Holy One Blessed
  is He!

In the house in Newark Blessed is He! In the madhouse Blessed
  is He! In the house of Death Blessed is He!

Blessed be He in homosexuality! Blessed be He in Paranoia!
  Blessed be He in the city! Blessed be He in the Book!

Blessed be He who dwells in the shadow! Blessed be He! Blessed
  be He!

Blessed be you Naomi in tears! Blessed be you Naomi in fears!
  Blessed Blessed Blessed in sickness!

Blessed be you Naomi in Hospitals! Blessed be you Naomi in
  solitude! Blest be your triumph! Blest be your bars! Blest be
  your last years' loneliness!

Blest be your failure! Blest be your stroke! Blest be the close of
  your eye! Blest be the gaunt of your cheek! Blest be your
  withered thighs!

Blessed be Thee Naomi in Death! Blessed be Death! Blessed be
  Death!

Blessed be He Who leads all sorrow to Heaven! Blessed be He
  in the end!

Blessed be He who builds Heaven in Darkness! Blessed Blessed
  Blessed be He! Blessed be He! Blessed be Death on us All!

ALLEN GINSBERG 257

Only to have not forgotten the beginning in which she drank
cheap sodas in the morgues of Newark,

only to have seen her weeping on gray tables in long wards of
her universe

only to have known the weird ideas of Hitler at the door, the
wires in her head, the three big sticks

rammed down her back, the voices in the ceiling shrieking out
her ugly early lays for 30 years,

only to have seen the time-jumps, memory lapse, the crash of
wars, the roar and silence of a vast electric shock,

only to have seen her painting crude pictures of Elevateds run-
ning over the rooftops of the Bronx

her brothers dead in Riverside or Russia, her lone in Long Island
writing a last letter—and her image in the sunlight at the
window

'The key is in the sunlight at the window in the bars the key is
in the sunlight,'

only to have come to that dark night on iron bed by stroke when
the sun gone down on Long Island

and the vast Atlantic roars outside the great call of Being to its
own

to come back out of the Nightmare—divided creation—with
her head lain on a pillow of the hospital to die

—in one last glimpse—all Earth one everlasting Light in the
familiar blackout—no tears for this vision—

But that the key should be left behind—at the window—the key
in the sunlight—to the living—that can take

that slice of light in hand—and turn the door—and look back see

Creation glistening backwards to the same grave, size of uni-
verse,

size of the tick of the hospital's clock on the archway over the
white door—

IV

O mother
what have I left out

O mother
what have I forgotten
O mother
farewell
with a long black shoe
farewell
with Communist Party and a broken stocking
farewell
with six dark hairs on the wen of your breast
farewell
with your old dress and a long black beard around the vagina
farewell
with your sagging belly
with your fear of Hitler
with your mouth of bad short stories
with your fingers of rotten mandolins
with your arms of fat Paterson porches
with your belly of strikes and smokestacks
with your chin of Trotsky and the Spanish War
with your voice singing for the decaying overbroken workers
with your nose of bad lay with your nose of the smell of the
  pickles of Newark
with your eyes
with your eyes of Russia
with your eyes of no money
with your eyes of false China
with your eyes of Aunt Elanor
with your eyes of starving India
with your eyes pissing in the park
with your eyes of America taking a fall
with your eyes of your failure at the piano
with your eyes of your relatives in California
with your eyes of Ma Rainey dying in an aumbulance
with your eyes of Czechoslovakia attacked by robots
with your eyes going to painting class at night in the Bronx
with your eyes of the killer Grandma you see on the horizon
  from the Fire-Escape

with your eyes running naked out of the apartment screaming
    into the hall
with your eyes being led away by policemen to an aumbulance
with your eyes strapped down on the operating table
with your eyes with the pancreas removed
with your eyes of appendix operation
with your eyes of abortion
with your eyes of ovaries removed
with your eyes of shock
with your eyes of lobotomy
with your eyes of divorce
with your eyes of stroke
with your eyes alone
with your eyes
with your eyes
with your Death full of Flowers

v

Caw caw caw crows shriek in the white sun over grave stones
    in Long Island
Lord Lord Lord Naomi underneath this grass my halflife and my
    own as hers
caw caw my eye be buried in the same Ground where I stand
    in Angel
Lord Lord great Eye that stares on All and moves in a black cloud
caw caw strange cry of Beings flung up into sky over the waving
    trees
Lord Lord O Grinder of giant Beyonds my voice in a boundless
    field in Sheol
Caw caw the call of Time rent out of foot and wing an instant
    in the universe
Lord Lord an echo in the sky the wind through ragged leaves the
    roar of memory
caw caw all years my birth a dream caw caw New York the bus
    the broken shoe the vast highschool caw caw all Visions of the
    Lord

Lord Lord Lord caw caw caw Lord Lord Lord caw caw caw
  Lord

AFTER YEATS

Now incense fills the air
and delight follows delight,
quiet supper in the carpet room,
music twangling from the Orient to my ear,
old friends at rest on bright mattresses,
old paintings on the walls, old poetry
thought anew, laughing at a mystic toy
statue painted gold, tea on the white table.

UPTOWN

Yellow-lit Budweiser signs over oaken bars,
"I've seen everything"—the bartender handing me change of
  $10,
I stared at him amiably eyes thru an obvious Adamic beard—
with Montana musicians homeless in Manhattan, teenage
curly hair themselves—we sat at the antique booth &
  gossiped,
Madame Grady's literary salon a curious value in New
  York—
"If I had my way I'd cut off your hair and send you to
  Vietnam"—
"Bless you then" I replied to a hatted thin citizen hurrying to
  the barroom door
upon wet dark Amsterdam Avenue decades later—
"And if I couldn't do that I'd cut your throat" he snarled
  farewell,
and "Bless you sir" I added as he went to his fate in the rain,
  dapper Irishman.

JAMES MERRILL

James Merrill appears to have led a charmed life, and so he seems the odd man out in a generation of artists characterized by instability. Poised, wealthy, cherished by a wide circle of admiring friends, and showered with numerous honors, he experienced his share of sorrow and despair, as the work makes clear, but on balance his career was an enviable one.

Born March 3, 1926, in New York City, the son of Charles E. Merrill, a founder of the investment firm of Merrill, Lynch, Pierce, Fenner, and Smith, he came into the world possessing not just the proverbial silver spoon but an entire place setting. He began writing a poem a day while attending the exclusive Lawrenceville School in Princeton. His parents, however, divorced when he was twelve (the "other woman" shows up in the poetry), and the traumatic event impinged on his seemingly carefree life. Adding to his personal distress was the growing recognition of his homosexuality, something, it was widely believed at the time, that under no circumstances should be revealed. It was not until years later that he was able to write candidly about his intimate feelings. He documents his youthful struggles most openly in an eloquent, refreshingly comic memoir called *A Different Person,* published in 1993.

At Amherst College he discovered Wallace Stevens as well as Marcel Proust, the subject of his honors thesis. He served in the army and later did some teaching, but for the most part he has devoted himself to a life of writing, punctuated with a good deal of traveling. His home base was Stonington, Connecticut; for many years he also spent time in Athens, and more recently he established a second residence in Key West. His companion of twenty-five years, David Jackson, is the "DJ" of his major opus, *The Changing Light at Sandover,* a vast dramatic work allegedly dictated to the two of them as they sat, night after night, at a Ouija board in Stonington.

The pre-*Sandover* work consists of lyrical poems, fiction (*The Seraglio* and *The (Diblos) Notebook*), and plays (*The Immortal Husband* and, in one act, *The Bait*). The books of lyrics and personal narratives, each characterized by technical legerdemain, include *Nights and Days,* winner of the National Book Award; *Braving the Elements,* recipient of the Bollingen Award; and *Divine Comedies,* awarded a Pulitzer Prize. In 1992 he brought out *Selected Poems, 1946–1985,* an essential companion for anyone attracted to his voice.

Certain words irresistibly come to mind when one considers this particular craftsman—words like urbane, playful, idiosyncratic, decorative, elegant, painterly, witty, puzzling, and entertaining. But since such a list may suggest little more than a brilliantly polished surface, I hasten to add that the work also reveals intriguing contradictions. Merrill can be sentimental and ironic, precious and robust, mercurial and accessible, elegiac and buoyant, literary and colloquial, companionable and aloof, sensual and solitary, silly and wise. What he never can be is vulgar or careless. Thoroughly in love with language—more interested, as one critic put it, in syntax than in sin—he did with words what Mozart did with notes.

In *A History of Modern Poetry,* David Perkins calls *The Changing Light at Sandover* one of the five most significant American long poems since Whitman. Such a judgment may be inflated (is it really superior to, say, Williams's *Paterson?*), but there can be no argument about the work's eccentricity and length. The three books and closing coda come to 560 pages, each one filled with elaborate wordplay. The twenty-six sections of the first book open with words that follow the course of the alphabet from A to Z, while the second uses mathematics as its organizing principle, and the third, filled with questions, has just three parts, titled "Yes," "&," and "No." The final word of the coda repeats the first word of the poem, bringing the work full circle. Within these rough outlines one hears an elaborate concert of voices, some from the living (Merrill, or "JM," and Jackson, "DJ"), the others—including those of W. H. Auden and his companion, Chester Kallman—ghostly presences speaking through the Ouija board. The work as a whole, preoccupied with the impact of science on moral faith, is, in Perkins's helpful words, a prolonged response to the sense of mortality. "Against this permeating awareness the humor of the poem—light, ebullient, witty, campy—has pathos and gallantry."

In *Late Settings,* published in 1985, and *The Inner Room,* 1988, Merrill returned to the self-contained short poem with clusters of lyrics simultaneously deeply felt and full of his customary playfulness. (*Late Settings* also contains "From the Cutting-Room Floor," made up of Ouija-evoked fragments involving Whitman, William Carlos Williams, and others cut from *Sandover.*) Merrill, at this point clearly a master in his prime, knew exactly what effects he wanted to achieve. In a reminiscence called "Days of 1941 and '44" he quotes from an early diary a reference to "heavenly colors and swell fish," and winces at this "Mismarriage of maternal gush / to regular-guy." He long since shed both gush and slang, developing in their place a diction both imaginative and precise, as in this description of a house fly:

> . . . the dull-red lacquer head
> Lifted from its socket, turned mechanically
> This way and that, like a wristwatch being wound,
> As if there would always be time. . . .

The double entendre in the final line is vintage Merrill—irrepressibly playful, he likes, in Robert Frost's phrase, to make words jump to the whack of his quip. A wrinkled sea cow, for example, is "Unmarriageable / (Unless to the Prince of Whales)," and ocean predators are "great sharkskin-suited criminals." He sees sunset as "Day's flush of pleasure, knowing its poem done," and a man who sires illegitimate children is—what else?—a "genetic litterbug."

Merrill's magic is especially evident in his control of rhythm and rhyme. He is able to do virtually anything with language, whether documenting Channel 13 in lines of thirteen syllables, exploiting conventional structures and inventing new ones (as in twenty-eight lines composed around just three rhymes), or shaping a stanza visually to underscore its subject. Like Auden, his principal mentor, he mastered the art of making complex constructions seem stylistically inevitable when in fact every detail has been polished to a high gloss. The results of this sleight of hand are lines that invite repeated scrutiny and that, to put it simply, are fun to read, whether silently or aloud. James Merrill died in 1995 at age 69.

The Changing Light at Sandover (Atheneum, 1983); *Selected Poems, 1946–1985* (Knopf, 1992); *A Different Person: A Memoir* (Knopf, 1993). For criticism, see Judith Moffett, *James Merrill: An Introduction to the Poetry* (Columbia University Press, 1984).

THE OCTOPUS

There are many monsters that a glassen surface
Restrains. And none more sinister
Than vision asleep in the eye's tight translucence.
Rarely it seeks now to unloose
Its diamonds. Having divined how drab a prison
The purest mortal tissue is,
Rarely it wakes. Unless, coaxed out by lusters
Extraordinary, like the octopus
From the gloom of its tank half-swimming half-drifting
Toward anything fair, a handkerchief
Or child's face dreaming near the glass, the writher
Advances in a godlike wreath
Of its own wrath. Chilled by such fragile reeling

A hundred blows of a boot-heel
Shall not quell, the dreamer wakes and hungers.
Percussive pulses, drum or gong,
Build in his skull their loud entrancement,
Volutions of a Hindu dance.
His hands move clumsily in the first conventional
Gestures of assent.
He is willing to undergo the volition and fervor
Of many fleshlike arms, observe
These in their holiness of indirection
Destroy, adore, evolve, reject—
Till on glass rigid with his own seizure
At length the sucking jewels freeze.

A RENEWAL

Having used every subterfuge
To shake you, lies, fatigue, or even that of passion,
Now I see no way but a clean break.
I add that I am willing to bear the guilt.

You nod assent. Autumn turns windy, huge,
A clear vase of dry leaves vibrating on and on.
We sit, watching. When I next speak
Love buries itself in me, up to the hilt.

A VISION OF THE GARDEN

One winter morning as a child
Upon the windowpane's thin frost I drew
Forehead and eyes and mouth the clear and mild
Features of nobody I knew

And then abstracted looking through
This or that wet transparent line

Beyond beheld a winter garden so
Heavy with snow its hedge of pine

And sun so brilliant on the snow
I breathed my pleasure out onto the chill pane
Only to see its angel fade in mist.
I was a child, I did not know

That what I longed for would resist
Neither what cold lines should my finger trace
On colder grounds before I found anew
In yours the features of that face

Whose words whose looks alone undo
Such frosts I lay me down in love in fear
At how they melt become a blossoming pear
Joy outstretched in our bodies' place.

CHILDLESSNESS

The weather of this winter night, my dream-wife
Ranting and raining, wakes me. Her cloak blown back
To show the lining's dull lead foil
Sweeps along asphalt. Houses
Look blindly on; one glimmers through a blind.
Outside, I hear her tricklings
Arraign my little plot:
Had it or not agreed
To transplantation for the common good
Of certain rare growths yielding guaranteed
Gold pollen, gender of suns, large, hardy,
Enviable blooms? But in my garden
Nothing's been seeded. Neither
Is that glimmering window mine.
I lie and think about the rain,
How it has been drawn up from the impure ocean,

From gardens lightly, deliberately tainted;
How it falls back, time after time,
Through poisons visible at sunset
When the enchantress, masked as friend, unfurls
Entire bolts of voluminous pistachio,
Saffron, and rose.
These, as I fall back to sleep,
And other slow colors clothe me, glide
To rest, then burst along my limbs like buds,
Like bombs from the navigator's vantage,
Waking me, lulling me. Later I am shown
The erased metropolis reassembled
On sampans, freighted each
With toddlers, holy dolls, dead ancestors.
One tiny monkey puzzles over fruit.
The vision rises and falls, the garland
Gently takes root
In the sea's coma. Hours go by
Before I can stand to own
A sky stained red, a world
Clad only in rags, threadbare,
Dabbling the highway's ice with blood.
A world. The cloak thrown down for it to wear
In token of past servitude
Has fallen onto the shoulders of my parents
Whom it is eating to the bone.

CHARLES ON FIRE

Another evening we sprawled about discussing
Appearances. And it was the consensus
That while uncommon physical good looks
Continued to launch one, as before, in life
(Among its vaporous eddies and false calms),
Still, as one of us said into his beard,
"Without your intellectual and spiritual

Values, man, you are sunk." No one but squared
The shoulders of his own unloveliness.
Long-suffering Charles, having cooked and served the meal,
Now brought out little tumblers finely etched
He filled with amber liquor and then passed.
"Say," said the same young man, "in Paris, France,
They do it this way"—bounding to his feet
And touching a lit match to our host's full glass.
A blue flame, gentle, beautiful, came, went
Above the surface. In a hush that fell
We heard the vessel crack. The contents drained
As who should step down from a crystal coach.
Steward of spirits, Charles's glistening hand
All at once gloved itself in eeriness.
The moment passed. He made two quick sweeps and
Was flesh again. "It couldn't matter less,"
He said, but with a shocked, unconscious glance
Into the mirror. Finding nothing changed,
He filled a fresh glass and sank down among us.

THE BROKEN HOME

Crossing the street,
I saw the parents and the child
At their window, gleaming like fruit
With evening's mild gold leaf.

In a room on the floor below,
Sunless, cooler—a brimming
Saucer of wax, marbly and dim—
I have lit what's left of my life.

I have thrown out yesterday's milk
And opened a book of maxims.
The flame quickens. The word stirs.

Tell me, tongue of fire,
That you and I are as real
At least as the people upstairs.

My father, who had flown in World War I,
Might have continued to invest his life
In cloud banks well above Wall Street and wife.
But the race was run below, and the point was to win.

Too late now, I make out in his blue gaze
(Through the smoked glass of being thirty-six)
The soul eclipsed by twin black pupils, sex
And business; time was money in those days.

Each thirteenth year he married. When he died
There were already several chilled wives
In sable orbit—rings, cars, permanent waves.
We'd felt him warming up for a green bride.

He could afford it. He was "in his prime"
At three score ten. But money was not time.
When my parents were younger this was a popular act:
A veiled woman would leap from an electric, wine-dark car
To the steps of no matter what—the Senate or the Ritz
    Bar—
And bodily, at newsreel speed, attack

No matter whom—Al Smith or José Maria Sert
Or Clemenceau—veins standing out on her throat
As she yelled *War mongerer! Pig! Give us the vote!,*
And would have to be hauled away in her hobble skirt.

What had the man done? Oh, made history.
Her business (he had implied) was giving birth,
Tending the house, mending the socks.

Always that same old story—
Father Time and Mother Earth,
A marriage on the rocks.

One afternoon, red, satyr-thighed
Michael, the Irish setter, head
Passionately lowered, led
The child I was to a shut door. Inside,

Blinds beat sun from the bed.
The green-gold room throbbed like a bruise.
Under a sheet, clad in taboos
Lay whom we sought, her hair undone, outspread,

And of a blackness found, if ever now, in old
Engravings where the acid bit.
I must have needed to touch it
Or the whiteness—was she dead?
Her eyes flew open, startled strange and cold.
The dog slumped to the floor. She reached for me. I fled.

Tonight they have stepped out onto the gravel.
The party is over. It's the fall
Of 1931. They love each other still.

She: Charlie, I can't stand the pace.
He: Come on, honey—why, you'll bury us all!

A lead soldier guards my windowsill:
Khaki rifle, uniform, and face.
Something in me grows heavy, silvery, pliable.

How intensely people used to feel!
Like metal poured at the close of a proletarian novel,
Refined and glowing from the crucible,
I see those two hearts, I'm afraid,

Still. Cool here in the graveyard of good and evil,
They are even so to be honored and obeyed.

. . . Obeyed, at least, inversely. Thus
I rarely buy a newspaper, or vote.
To do so, I have learned, is to invite
The tread of a stone guest within my house.

Shooting this rusted bolt, though, against him,
I trust I am no less time's child than some
Who on the heath impersonate Poor Tom
Or on the barricades risk life and limb.

Nor do I try to keep a garden, only
An avocado in a glass of water—
Roots pallid, gemmed with air. And later,

When the small gilt leaves have grown
Fleshy and green, I let them die, yes, yes,
And start another. I am earth's no less.

A child, a red dog roam the corridors,
Still, of the broken home. No sound. The brilliant
Rag runners halt before wide-open doors.
My old room! Its wallpaper—cream, medallioned
With pink and brown—brings back the first nightmares,
Long summer colds, and Emma, sepia-faced,
Perspiring over broth carried upstairs
Aswim with golden fats I could not taste.

The real house became a boarding school.
Under the ballroom ceiling's allegory
Someone at last may actually be allowed
To learn something; or, from my window, cool
With the unstiflement of the entire story,
Watch a red setter stretch and sink in cloud.

THE MAD SCENE

Again last night I dreamed the dream called Laundry.
In it, the sheets and towels of a life we were going to share,
The milk-stiff bibs, the shroud, each rag to be ever
Trampled or soiled, bled on or groped for blindly,
Came swooning out of an enormous willow hamper
Onto moon-marbly boards. We had just met. I watched
From outer darkness. I had dressed myself in clothes
Of a new fiber that never stains or wrinkles, never
Wears thin. The opera house sparkled with tiers
And tiers of eyes, like mine enlarged by belladonna,
Trained inward. There I saw the cloud-clot, gust by gust,
Form, and the lightning bite, and the roan mane unloosen.
Fingers were running in panic over the flute's nine gates.
Why did I flinch? I loved you. And in the downpour
     laughed
To have us wrung white, gnarled together, one
Topmost mordent of wisteria,
As the lean tree burst into grief.

DAYS OF 1964

Houses, an embassy, the hospital,
Our neighborhood sun-cured if trembling still
In pools of the night's rain . . .
Across the street that led to the center of town
A steep hill kept one company part way
Or could be climbed in twenty minutes
For some literally breathtaking views,
Framed by umbrella pines, of city and sea.
Underfoot, cyclamen, autumn crocus grew
Spangled as with fine sweat among the relics
Of good times had by all. If not Olympus,
An out-of-earshot, year-round hillside revel.

I brought home flowers from my climbs.
Kyria Kleo who cleaned for us
Put them in water, sighing *Virgin, Virgin.*
Her legs hurt. She wore brown, was fat, past fifty,
And looked like a Palmyra matron
Copied in lard and horsehair. How she loved
You, me, loved us all, the bird, the cat!
I think now she *was* love. She sighed and glistened
All day with it, or pain, or both.
(We did not notably communicate.)
She lived nearby with her pious mother
And wastrel son. She called me her real son.

I paid her generously, I dare say.
Love makes one generous. Look at us. We'd known
Each other so briefly that instead of sleeping
We lay whole nights, open, in the lamplight,
And gazed, or traded stories.

One hour comes back—you gasping in my arms
With love, or laughter, or both,
I having just remembered and told you
What I'd looked up to see on my way downtown at noon:
Poor old Kleo, her aching legs,
Trudging into the pines. I called,
Called three times before she turned.
Above a tight, skyblue sweater, her face
Was painted. Yes. Her face was painted
Clown-white, white of the moon by daylight,
Lidded with pearl, mouth a poinsettia leaf,
Eat me, pay me—the erotic mask
Worn the world over by illusion
To weddings of itself and simple need.

Startled mute, we had stared—was love illusion?—
And gone our ways. Next, I was crossing a square
In which a moveable outdoor market's

Vegetables, chickens, pottery kept materializing
Through a dream-press of hagglers each at heart
Leery lest he be taken, plucked,
The bird, the flower of that November mildness,
Self lost up soft clay paths, or found, foothold,
Where the bud throbs awake
The better to be nipped, self on its knees in mud—
Here I stopped cold, for both our sakes;

And calmer on my way home bought us fruit.

Forgive me if you read this. (And may Kyria Kleo,
Should someone ever put it into Greek
And read it aloud to her, forgive me, too.)
I had gone so long without loving,
I hardly knew what I was thinking.

Where I hid my face, your touch, quick, merciful,
Blindfolded me. A god breathed from my lips.
If that was illusion, I wanted it to last long;
To dwell, for its daily pittance, with us there,
Cleaning and watering, sighing with love or pain.
I hoped it would climb when it needed to the heights
Even of degradation, as I for one
Seemed, those days, to be always climbing
Into a world of wild
Flowers, feasting, tears—or was I falling, legs
Buckling, heights, depths,
Into a pool of each night's rain?
But you were everywhere beside me, masked,
As who was not, in laughter, pain, and love.

KOSTAS TYMPAKIANÁKIS

Sit, friend. We'll be drinking and I'll tell you why.
Today I went to Customs to identify

My brother—it was him, all right, in spite of both
Feet missing from beneath his Army overcoat.

He was a handsome devil twice the size of me.
We're all good-looking in my family.
If you saw that brother, or what's left of him,
You'd understand at once the kind of man he'd been.

I have other brothers, one whose face I broke
In a family quarrel, and that's no joke:
I'm small but strong, when I get mad I fight.
Seven hundred vines of his were mine by right

And still are—fine! He's welcome to them.
I'm twenty-two. It's someone else's turn to dream.
I liked our school and teacher till they made me stop
And earn my living in a welder's shop.

Cousins and friends were learning jokes and games
At the Kafeneíon behind steamed-up panes.
I worked without a mask in a cold rain of sparks
That fell on you and burned—look, you can still see marks.

The German officer stubbed his *puro* out
On my mother's nipples but her mouth stayed shut.
She lived to bear me with one foot in the grave
And they never found my father in his mountain cave.

He died last year at eighty. To his funeral
Came a NATO Captain and an English General.
Our name is known around Herákleion
In all the hill towns, just ask anyone.

Outside our village up above Knossós
A railed-in plot of cypresses belongs to us,
Where we'll put my brother, and if there's room
One day I'll lie beside him till the crack of doom.

But I'd rather travel to a far-off land,
Though I never shall, and settle, do you understand?
The trouble here is not with sun and soil
So much as meanness in the human soul.

I worked a time in Germany, I saw a whore
Smile at me from inside her little lighted door.
She didn't want my money, she was kind and clean
With mirrors we submerged in like a submarine.

The girl I loved left me for a Rhodiot.
I should be broken-hearted but it's strange, I'm not.
Take me with you when you sail next week,
You'll see a different cosmos through the eyes of a Greek.

Or write my story down for people. Use my name.
And may it bring you all the wealth and fame
It hasn't brought its bearer. Here, let's drink our wine!
Who could have imagined such a life as mine?

THE VICTOR DOG

FOR ELIZABETH BISHOP

Bix to Buxtehude to Boulez,
The little white dog on the Victor label
Listens long and hard as he is able.
It's all in a day's work, whatever plays.

From judgment, it would seem, he has refrained.
He even listens earnestly to Bloch,
Then builds a church upon our acid rock.
He's man's—no—he's the Leiermann's best friend,

Or would be if hearing and listening were the same.
Does he hear? I fancy he rather smells
Those lemon-gold arpeggios in Ravel's
"Les jets d'eau du palais de ceux qui s'aiment."

He ponders the Schumann Concerto's tall willow hit
By lightning, and stays put. When he surmises
Through one of Bach's eternal boxwood mazes
The oboe pungent as a bitch in heat,

Or when the calypso decants its raw bay rum
Or the moon in *Wozzeck* reddens ripe for murder,
He doesn't sneeze or howl; just listens harder.
Adamant needles bear down on him from

Whirling of outer space, too black, too near—
But he was taught as a puppy not to flinch,
Much less to imitate his bête noire Blanche
Who barked, fat foolish creature, at King Lear.

Still others fought in the road's filth over Jezebel,
Slavered on hearths of horned and pelted barons.
His forebears lacked, to say the least, forbearance.
Can nature change in him? Nothing's impossible.

The last chord fades. The night is cold and fine.
His master's voice rasps through the grooves' bare groves.
Obediently, in silence like the grave's
He sleeps there on the still-warm gramophone

Only to dream he is at the première of a Handel
Opera long thought lost—*Il Cane Minore*.
Its allegorical subject is his story!
A little dog revolving round a spindle

Gives rise to harmonies beyond belief,
A cast of stars. . . . Is there in Victor's heart
No honey for the vanquished? Art is art.
The life it asks of us is a dog's life.

Lost in Translation

FOR RICHARD HOWARD

Diese Tage, die leer dir scheinen
und wertlos für das All,
haben Wurzeln zwischen den Steinen
und trinken dort überall.

A card table in the library stands ready
To receive the puzzle which keeps never coming.
Daylight shines in or lamplight down
Upon the tense oasis of green felt.
Full of unfulfillment, life goes on,
Mirage arisen from time's trickling sands
Or fallen piecemeal into place:
German lesson, picnic, see-saw, walk
With the collie who "did everything but talk"—
Sour windfalls of the orchard back of us.
A summer without parents is the puzzle,
Or should be. But the boy, day after day,
Writes in his Line-a-Day *No puzzle.*

He's in love, at least. His French Mademoiselle,
In real life a widow since Verdun,
Is stout, plain, carrot-haired, devout.
She prays for him, as does a curé in Alsace,
Sews costumes for his marionettes,
Helps him to keep behind the scene
Whose sidelit goosegirl, speaking with his voice,
Plays Guinevere as well as Gunmoll Jean.
Or else at bedtime in his tight embrace
Tells him her own French hopes, her German fears,
Her—but what more is there to tell?
Having known grief and hardship, Mademoiselle
Knows little more. Her languages. Her place.
Noon coffee. Mail. The watch that also waited
Pinned to her heart, poor gold, throws up its hands—

No puzzle! Steaming bitterness
Her sugars draw pops back into his mouth, translated:
"Patience, chéri. Geduld, mein Schatz."
(Thus, reading Valéry the other evening
And seeming to recall a Rilke version of "Palme,"
That sunlit paradigm whereby the tree
Taps a sweet wellspring of authority,
The hour came back. Patience dans l'azur.
Geduld im . . . Himmelblau? Mademoiselle.)

Out of the blue, as promised, of a New York
Puzzle-rental shop the puzzle comes—
A superior one, containing a thousand hand-sawn,
Sandal-scented pieces. Many take
Shapes known already—the craftsman's repertoire
Nice in its limitation—from other puzzles:
Witch on broomstick, ostrich, hourglass,
Even (surely not just in retrospect)
An inchling, innocently branching palm.
These can be put aside, made stories of
While Mademoiselle spreads out the rest face-up,
Herself excited as a child; or questioned
Like incoherent faces in a crowd,
Each with its scrap of highly colored
Evidence the Law must piece together.
Sky-blue ostrich? Likely story.
Mauve of the witch's cloak white, severed fingers
Pluck? Detain her. The plot thickens
As all at once two pieces interlock.

Mademoiselle does borders—(Not so fast.
A London dusk, December last.
Chatter silenced in the library
This grown man reenters, wearing grey.
A medium. All except him have seen
Panel slid back, recess explored,
An object at once unique and common

Displayed, planted in a plain tole
Casket the subject now considers
Through shut eyes, saying in effect:
"Even as voices reach me vaguely
A dry saw-shriek drowns them out,
Some loud machinery—a lumber mill?
Far uphill in the fir forest
Trees tower, tense with shock,
Groaning and cracking as they crash groundward.
But hidden here is a freak fragment
Of a pattern complex in appearance only.
What it seems to show is superficial
Next to that long-term lamination
Of hazard and craft, the karma that has
Made it matter in the first place.
Plywood, Piece of a puzzle." Applause
Acknowledged by an opening of lids
Upon the thing itself. A sudden dread—
But to go back. All this lay years ahead.)

Mademoiselle does borders. Straight-edge pieces
Align themselves with earth or sky
In twos and threes, naive cosmogonists
Whose views clash. Nomad inlanders meanwhile
Begin to cluster where the totem
Of a certain vibrant egg-yolk yellow
Or pelt of what emerging animal
Acts on the straggler like a trumpet call
To form a more sophisticated unit.
By suppertime two ragged wooden clouds
Have formed. In one, a Sheik with beard
And flashing sword hilt (he is all but finished)
Steps forward on a tiger skin. A piece
Snaps shut, and fangs gnash out at us!
In the second cloud—they gaze from cloud to cloud
With marked if undecipherable feeling—
Most of a dark-eyed woman veiled in mauve

Is being helped down from her camel (kneeling)
By a small backward-looking slave or page-boy
(Her son, thinks Mademoiselle mistakenly)
Whose feet have not been found. But lucky finds
In the last minutes before bed
Anchor both factions to the scene's limits
And, by so doing, orient
Them eye to eye across the green abyss.
The yellow promises, oh bliss,
To be in time a sumptuous tent.

Puzzle begun I write in the day's space,
Then, while she bathes, peek at Mademoiselle's
Page to the curé: ". . . cette innocente mère,
Ce pauvre enfant, que deviendront-ils?"
Her azure script is curlicued like pieces
Of the puzzle she will be telling him about.
(Fearful incuriosity of childhood!
"Tu as l'accent allemand," said Dominique.
Indeed. Mademoiselle was only French by marriage.
Child of an English mother, a remote
Descendant of the great explorer Speke,
And Prussian father. No one knew. I heard it
Long afterwards from her nephew, a UN
Interpreter. His matter-of-fact account
Touched old strings. My poor Mademoiselle,
With 1939 about to shake
This world where "each was the enemy, each the friend"
To its foundations, kept, though signed in blood,
Her peace a shameful secret to the end.)
"Schlaf wohl, chéri." Her kiss. Her thumb
Crossing my brow against the dreams to come.

This World that shifts like sand, its unforeseen
Consolidations and elate routine,
Whose Potentate had lacked a retinue?
Lo! it assembles on the shrinking Green.

Gunmetal-skinned or pale, all plumes and scars,
Of Vassalage the noblest avatars—
The very coffee-bearer in his vair
Vest is a swart Highness, next to ours.

Kef easing Boredom, and iced syrups, thirst,
In guessed-at glooms old wives who know the worst
Outsweat that virile fiction of the New:
"Insh'Allah, he will tire—" "—or kill her first!"

(Hardly a proper subject for the Home,
Work of—dear Richard, I shall let *you* comb
Archives and learned journals for his name—
A minor lion attending on Gérôme.)

While, thick as Thebes whose presently complete
Gates close behind them, Houri and Afreet
Both claim the Page. He wonders whom to serve,
And what his duties are, and where his feet,

And if we'll find, as some before us did,
That piece of Distance deep in which lies hid
Your tiny apex sugary with sun,
Eternal Triangle, Great Pyramid!

Then Sky alone is left, a hundred blue
Fragments in revolution, with no clue
To where a Niche will open. Quite a task,
Putting together Heaven, yet we do.

It's done. Here under the table all along
Were those missing feet. It's done.

The dog's tail thumping. Mademoiselle sketching
Costumes for a coming harem drama
To star the goosegirl. All too soon the swift
Dismantling. Lifted by two corners,

The puzzle hung together—and did not.
Irresistibly a populace
Unstitched of its attachments, rattled down.
Power went to pieces as the witch
Slithered easily from Virtue's gown.
The blue held out for time, but crumbled, too.
The city had long fallen, and the tent,
A separating sauce mousseline,
Been swept away. Remained the green
On which the grown-ups gambled. A green dusk.
First lightning bugs. Last glow of west
Green in the false eyes of (coincidence)
Our mangy tiger safe on his bared hearth.

Before the puzzle was boxed and readdressed
To the puzzle shop in the mid-Sixties,
Something tells me that one piece contrived
To stay in the boy's pocket. How do I know?
I know because so many later puzzles
Had missing pieces—Maggie Teyte's high notes
Gone at the war's end, end of the vogue for collies,
A house torn down; and hadn't Mademoiselle
Kept back her pitiful bit of truth as well?
I've spent the last days, furthermore,
Ransacking Athens for that translation of "Palme."
Neither the Goethehaus nor the National Library
Seems able to unearth it. Yet I can't
Just be imagining. I've seen it. Know
How much of the sun-ripe original
Felicity Rilke made himself forego
(Who loved French words—verger, mûr, parfumer)
In order to render its underlying sense.
Know already in that tongue of his
What Pains, what monolithic Truths
Shadow stanza to stanza's symmetrical
Rhyme-rutted pavement. Know that ground plan left
Sublime and barren, where the warm Romance

Stone by stone faded, cooled; the fluted nouns
Made taller, lonelier than life
By leaf-carved capitals in the afterglow.
The owlet umlaut peeps and hoots
Above the open vowel. And after rain
A deep reverberation fills with stars.

Lost, is it, buried? One more missing piece?

But nothing's lost. Or else: all is translation
And every bit of us is lost in it
(Or found—I wander through the ruin of S
Now and then, wondering at the peacefulness)
And in that loss a self-effacing tree,
Color of context, imperceptibly
Rustling with its angel, turns the waste
To shade and fiber, milk and memory.

THE PIER: UNDER PISCES

The shallows, brighter,
Wetter than water,
Tepidly glitter with the fingerprint-
Obliterating feel of kerosene.

Each piling like a totem
Rises from rock bottom
Straight through the ceiling
Aswirl with suns, clear ones or pale bluegreen,

And beyond! where bubbles burst,
Sphere of their worst dreams,
If dream is what they do,
These floozy fish—

Ceramic-lipped in filmy
Peekaboo blouses,

Fluorescent body
Stockings, hot stripes,

Swayed by the hypnotic ebb and flow
Of supermarket Muzak,
Bolero beat the undertow's
Pebble-filled gourds repeat;

Jailbait consumers of subliminal
Hints dropped from on high
In gobbets none
Eschews as minced kin;

Who, hooked themselves—bamboo diviner
Bent their way
Vigorously nodding
Encouragement—

Are one by one hauled kisswise, oh
Into some blinding hell
Policed by leathery ex-
Justices each

Minding his catch, if catch is what he can,
If mind is what one means—
The torn mouth
Stifled by newsprint, working still. If . . . if . . .

The little scales
Grow stiff. Dusk plugs her dryer in,
Buffs her nails, riffles through magazines,
While far and wide and deep

Rove the great sharkskin-suited criminals
And safe in this lit shrine
A boy sits. He'll be eight.
We've drunk our milk, we've eaten our stringbeans,

But left untasted on the plate
The fish. An eye, a broiled pearl, meeting mine,
I lift his fork . . .
The bite. The tug of fate.

THE SCHOOL PLAY

"Harry of Hereford, Lancaster, and Derby,
Stands here for God, his country, and . . . " And what?
"Stands here for God, his Sovereign, and himself,"
Growled Captain Fry who had the play by heart.
I was the First Herald, "a small part"
—I was small too—"but an important one."
What was not important to the self
At nine or ten? Already I had crushes
On Mowbray, Bushy, and the Duke of York.
Handsome Donald Niemann (now himself,
According to the Bulletin, headmaster
Of his own school somewhere out West) awoke
Too many self-indulgent mouthings in
The dummy mirror before smashing it,
For me to set my scuffed school cap at him.
Another year I'd play that part myself,
Or Puck, or Goneril, or Prospero.
Later, in adolescence, it was thought
Clever to speak of having found oneself,
With a smile and rueful headshake for those who hadn't.
People still do. Only the other day
A woman my age told us that her son
"Hadn't found himself"—at thirty-one!
I heard in the mind's ear an amused hum
Of mothers and fathers from beyond the curtain,
And that flushed, far-reaching hour came back
Months of rehearsal in the gymnasium
Had led to: when the skinny nobodies
Who'd memorized the verse and learned to speak it

Emerged in beards and hose (or gowns and rouge)
Vivid with character, having put themselves
All unsuspecting into the masters' hands.

THE HOUSE FLY

Come October, if I close my eyes,
A self till then subliminal takes flight
Buzzing round me, settling upon the knuckle,
The lip to be explored not as in June
But with a sense verging on micromania
Of wrong, of tiny, hazy, crying wrongs
Which quite undo her—look at that zigzag totter,
Proboscis blindly tapping like a cane.
Gone? If so, only to re-alight

Or else in a stray beam resume the grand toilette
(Eggs of next year's mischief long since laid):
Unwearying strigils taken to the frayed,
Still glinting wings; the dull-red lacquer head
Lifted from its socket, turned mechanically
This way and that, like a wristwatch being wound,
As if there would always be time . . .

Downstairs in this same house one summer night,
Founding the cult, her ancestress alit
On the bare chest of Strato Mouflouzélis
Who stirred in the lamp-glow but did not wake.
To say so brings it back on every autumn
Feebler wings, and further from that Sun,
That mist-white wafer she and I partake of
Alone this afternoon, making a rite
Distinct from both the blessing and the blight.

INDEX OF TITLES

INDEX OF FIRST LINES

Sing in me, Muse,
and through me tell the story...

—Homer, *The Odyssey*

Jaguar of Sweet Laughter　　0-679-74304-9　$11.00 (Can. $14.50)
　by Diane Ackerman

Collected Poems　　0-679-73197-0　$22.50 (Can. $30.00)
　by W. H. Auden

Selected Poems　　0-679-72483-4　$11.00 (Can. $14.00)
　by W. H. Auden

Ultramarine　　0-394-75535-9　$11.00 (Can. $14.00)
　by Raymond Carver

Where Water Comes Together　　0-394-74327-X　$8.95 (Can. $11.95)
　with Other Water
　by Raymond Carver

Six American Poets:　　0-679-74525-4　$13.00 (Can. $17.95)
　Walt Whitman,
　Emily Dickinson, Wallace Stevens,
　William Carlos Williams,
　Robert Frost, Langston Hughes
　edited by Joel Conarroe

Divine Comedy　　0-394-70126-7　$10.00 (Can. $13.00)
　by Dante Alighieri,
　translated by John Aitken Carlyle,
　Thomas Okey, and Philip H. Wickseed

The Ink Dark Moon:　　0-679-72958-5　$10.00 (Can. $12.50)
　Love Poems by Ono no
　Komachi and Izumi Shikibu,
　Women of the Ancient Court of Japan
　translated by Jane Hirshfield with
　Mariko Aratani

The Odyssey　　0-679-72813-9　$8.00 (Can. $10.00)
　by Homer, translated by
　Robert Fitzgerald

The Panther and the Lash *by Langston Hughes*	0-679-73659-X	$10.00 (Can. $12.50)
Selected Poems of Langston Hughes	0-679-72818-X	$10.00 (Can. $12.50)
Selected Poetry *by Robinson Jeffers*	0-394-70295-6	$7.00 (Can. $9.50)
Sleeping on the Wing *by Kenneth Koch*	0-394-74364-4	$10.00 (Can. $13.50)
The Unicorn and Other Poems *by Anne Morrow Lindbergh*	0-394-71822-4	$6.00 (Can. $7.50)
The Vintage Book of Contemporary American Poetry *edited by J. D. McClatchy*	0-679-72858-9	$15.00 (Can. $19.00)
Selected Poems *by Frank O'Hara*	0-394-71973-5	$16.00 (Can. $20.00)
The Colossus and Other Poems *by Sylvia Plath*	0-394-70466-5	$7.00 (Can. $9.00)
Selected Poetry *by Rainer Maria Rilke*	0-679-72201-7	$12.00 (Can. $15.00)
All You Who Sleep Tonight *by Vikram Seth*	0-679-73025-7	$7.00 (Can. $9.50)
The Golden Gate *a novel in verse by Vikram Seth*	0-679-73457-0	$12.00 (Can. $16.00)
Collected Poems *by Wallace Stevens*	0-679-72669-1	$15.00 (Can. $19.00)
Opus Posthumous *by Wallace Stevens*	0-679-72534-2	$14.95 (Can. $20.00)
The Palm at the End of the Mind *by Wallace Stevens*	0-679-72445-1	$11.00 (Can. $14.50)
The Aeneid *by Virgil, translated by Robert Fitzgerald*	0-679-72952-6	$8.00 (Can. $10.00)

VINTAGE BOOKS

AVAILABLE AT YOUR LOCAL BOOKSTORE, OR CALL TOLL-FREE TO ORDER: 1-800-733-3000 (CREDIT CARDS ONLY). PRICES SUBJECT TO CHANGE.